Journal of International Business

Management International Review

Special Issue 1/2003

Editorial

Bent Petersen (Guest Editor)
International Management and the Internet – Post-hype

Guest Editor's Introduction

Bent Petersen/Lawrence S. Welch
International Business Development and the Internet

Rajesh Chakrabarti/Barry Scholnick
Frictions in International E-Commerce

Thomas C. Lawton/Steven M. McGuire
Governing E-Commerce

Steven Globerman
E-Business and Global Sourcing

Denice E. Welch/Verner Worm/Marilyn Fenwick
Are Virtual International Assignments Feasible?

Volker Mahnke/Markus Venzin
Internationalization of Digital Information Good Providers

D 21247

GABLER

ISBN 978-3-409-12389-1 ISBN 978-3-663-01562-8 (eBook)
DOI 10.1007/978-3-663-01562-8

EDITORIAL BOARD

Professor Raj Aggarwal, Kent State University, Kent – U.S.A.
Professor Jeffrey S. Arpan, University of South Carolina, Columbia – U.S.A.
Professor Daniel van Den Bulcke, Universiteit Antwerpen – Belgium
Professor John A. Cantwell, University of Reading – United Kingdom
Professor S. Tamer Cavusgil, Michigan State University, East Lansing – U.S.A.
Professor Frederick D.S. Choi, New York University – U.S.A.
Professor Farok Contractor, Rutgers University, Newark – U.S.A.
Professor John D. Daniels, University of Miami, Coral Gables – U.S.A.
Professor Peter J. Dowling, University of Canberra – Australia
Professor Santiago García Echevarría, Universidad de Alcála de Henares, Madrid – Spain
Professor Lawrence A. Gordon, University of Maryland, College Park – U.S.A.
Professor Sidney J. Gray, University of New South Wales, Sydney – Australia
Professor Geir Gripsrud, Norwegian School of Management, Sandvika – Norway
Professor Jean-François Hennart, Tilburg University – The Netherlands
Professor Georges Hirsch, Centre Franco-Vietnamien de Formation à la gestion, Paris – France
Professor Neil Hood, University of Strathclyde, Glasgow – United Kingdom
Professor Andrew Inkpen, Thunderbird, The American Graduate School of International Management, Glendale – U.S.A.
Professor Eugene D. Jaffe, Bar-Ilan University, Ramat-Gan – Israel
Professor Erdener Kaynak, Pennsylvania State University, Middletown – U.S.A.
Professor Yui Kimura, University of Tsukuba, Tokyo – Japan
Professor Michael Kutschker, Katholische Universität Eichstätt, Ingolstadt – Germany
Professor Reijo Luostarinen, Helsinki School of Economics – Finland
Professor Klaus Macharzina, Universität Hohenheim, Stuttgart – Germany
Professor Roger Mansfield, Cardiff Business School – United Kingdom
Professor Mark Mendenhall, University of Tennessee, Chattanooga – U.S.A.
Professor Rolf Mirus, University of Alberta, Edmonton – Canada
Professor Michael H. Moffett, American Graduate School, Phoenix – U.S.A.
Professor Krzysztof Y. Obloj, University of Warsaw – Poland
Professor Lars Oxelheim, Lund University – Sweden
Professor Ki-An Park, Kyung Hee University, Seoul – Korea
Professor Robert D. Pearce, University of Reading – United Kingdom
Professor Lee Radebaugh, Brigham Young University, Provo – U.S.A.
Professor Wolf Reitsperger, Universität Hamburg – Germany
Professor Edwin Rühli, Universität Zürich – Switzerland
Professor Alan M. Rugman, Indiana University, Bloomington, U.S.A.
Professor Rakesh B. Sambharya, Rutgers University, Camden, U.S.A.
Professor Reinhart Schmidt, Universität Halle-Wittenberg – Germany
Professor Hans Schöllhammer, University of California, Los Angeles – U.S.A.
Professor Oded Shenkar, The Ohio State University, Columbus – U.S.A.
Professor Vitor Corado Simoes, Universidade Técnica de Lisboa – Portugal
Professor John Stopford, 6 Chalcot Square, London NW1 8YB – United Kingdom
Professor Daniel P. Sullivan, University of Delaware, Newark – U.S.A.
Professor Norihiko Suzuki, International Christian University, Tokyo – Japan
Professor Stephen Bruce Tallmann, University of Utah, Salt Lake City – U.S.A.
Professor George Tesar, Umeå University, Umeå – Sweden
Professor José de la Torre, Florida International University, Miami – U.S.A.
Professor Rosalie L. Tung, Simon Fraser University, Burnaby, BC – Canada
Professor Jean-Claude Usunier, University of Lousanne, Lousanne – Dorigny – Switzerland
Professor Alain Charles Verbeke, Vrije Universiteit Brussel – Belgium
Professor Lawrence S. Welch, Mt Eliza Business School, Melbourne, Australia
Professor Martin K. Welge, Universität Dortmund – Germany
Professor Bernard Yin Yeung, New York University – U.S.A.
Professor Masaru Yoshimori, Yokohama National University – Japan

BOOK REVIEW EDITOR

Professor Dr. Johann Engelhard, Universität Bamberg – Germany

EDITOR

MANAGEMENT INTERNATIONAL REVIEW, *Professor Dr. Profs. h.c. Dr. h.c. Klaus Macharzina, Universität Hohenheim (510 E), Schloss-Osthof-Ost, D-70599 Stuttgart, Germany, Tel. (0711) 4 59-29 08, Fax (0711) 459-3288, E-mail: klausmac@uni-hohenheim.de, Internet: http://www.uni-hohenheim.de/~mir Assistant Editors: Professor Dr. Michael-Jörg Oesterle, Universität Bremen, Germany, Professor Dr. Joachim Wolf, Universität Kiel, Germany, Editorial office: Mrs. Sylvia Ludwig*

VOLUME 43 · SPECIAL ISSUE · 2003/1

CONTENTS

Guest Editor's Introduction 3
Bent Petersen/Lawrence S. Welch
International Business Development and the Internet, Post-hype . . 7
Rajesh Chakrabarti/Barry Scholnick
Frictions in International E-Commerce 31
Thomas C. Lawton/Steven M. McGuire
Governing the Electronic Market Space: Appraising the Apparent Global Consensus on E-Commerce Self-regulation 51
Steven Globerman
E-Business and Global Sourcing – Inferences from Securities Exchanges 73
Denice E. Welch/Verner Worm/Marilyn Fenwick
Are Virtual International Assignments Feasible? 95
Volker Mahnke/Markus Venzin
The Internationalization Process of Digital Information Good Providers 115

GUIDELINE FOR AUTHORS

mir welcomes articles on original theoretical contributions, empirical research, state-of-the-art surveys or reports on recent developments in the areas of

a) International Business b) Transnational Corporations c) Intercultural Management d) Strategic Management e) Business Policy.

Manuscripts are reviewed with the understanding that they are substantially new, have not been previously published in whole (including book chapters) or in part (including exhibits), have not been previously accepted for publication, are not under consideration by any other publisher, and will not be submitted elsewhere until a decision is reached regarding their publication in **mir**. The only exception is papers in conference proceedings, which we treat as work-in-progress.

Contributions should be submitted in English language in a Microsoft or compatible format by e-mail to the Editor at klausmac@uni-hohenheim.de. The complete text including the references, tables and figures should as a rule not exceed 25 pages in a usual setting (approximately *7000 words*). Reply papers should normally not exceed 1500 words. The title page should include the following elements: Author(s) name, Heading of the article, Abstract (two sections of about 30 words each), Key Results (20 words), Author's line (author's name, academic title, position and affiliation) and on the bottom a proposal for an abbreviated heading on the front cover of the journal.

Submitted papers must be written according to mir's formal guidelines. Only those manuscripts can enter the reviewing process which adhere to our guidelines. Authors are requested to

- use *endnotes* for clarification sparingly. References to the literature are indicated in the text by author's name and year of publication in parentheses, e.g. (Reitsperger/Daniel 1990, p. 210, Eiteman 1989). The references should be listed in alphabetical order at the end of the text. They should include full bibliographical details and be cited in the following manner: e.g.

    Reitsperger, W. D./Daniel, S. J., Dynamic Manufacturing: A Comparison of Attitudes in the U.S. and Japan, *Management International Review*, 30, 1990, pp. 203–216.

    Eiteman, D. K., Financial Sourcing, in Macharzina, K./Welge, M. K. (eds.), *Handwörterbuch Export und Internationale Unternehmung*, Stuttgart: Poeschel 1989, pp. 602–621.

    Stopford, J. M./Wells, L. T. Jr., *Managing the Multinational Enterprise*, New York: Basic Books 1972.

- avoid *terms* that may be interpreted denigrating to ethnic or other groups.
- be especially careful in dealing with gender. Traditional customs such as "... the manager wishes that **his** interest ..." can favor the acceptance of inequality were none exist. The use of plural pronouns is preferred. If this is impossible, the term "he or she" or "he/she" can be used.

In the case of publication authors are supplied one complimentary copy of the issue and 30 off-prints free of charge. Additional copies may be ordered *prior to printing*. Overseas shipment is by boat; air-delivery will be charged extra.

The author agrees, that his/her article is published not only in this journal but that it can also be reproduced by the publisher and his licensees through license agreement in other journals (also in translated versions), through reprint in omnibus volumes (i.e. for anniversary editions of the journal or the publisher or in subject volumes), through longer extracts in books of the publisher also for advertising purposes, through multiplication and distribution on CD ROM or other data media, through storage on data bases, their transmission and retrieval, during the time span of the copyright laws on the article at home and abroad.

Editorial

© Gabler Verlag 2003

Guest Editor's Introduction

"International Management and the Internet – Post-hype" is the title of this special issue of **mir**. Three years after the burst of the dot-com bubble in the stock exchange markets some **mir** readers might find that a special issue on the Internet and international management exposes a sense of timing just slightly better than delivering on-line ordered Christmas merchandise after New Year's Eve. Some might suspect that the timing is explained by an extremely long review process. The inclusion of the word "post-hype" in the title, however, should obviate such thoughts inasmuch as it indicates that even though Internet business (including e-business) no longer makes headlines, the Internet does affect the management of international business operations in ways that to a large extent remain unresolved. Hence, it seems due time to reflect on the basis of the empirical evidence of the last 7–8 years during which firms have pursued the commercial opportunities of the Internet. The e-business hype of the 1990s generated a wealth of predictions about how the new information and communication technology (I&CT) would change the organisational forms and the ways business transactions would be conducted. In particular, international business was expected to undergo a dramatic transformation, even to the extent where the words "international" and "localisation" would disappear from business managers' vocabulary – replaced by terms like "the borderless market space" and "the global digital network". Clearly, reality has not matched the hype. But the Internet transformation of international business management may still be significant. In other words, international management scholars and practitioners alike have a genuine interest in reassessing where the Internet "revolution" has taken international business management so far. The aim of this special issue is to contribute to this reassessment.

The call for papers prompted submission of sixteen papers (this, somewhat modest response, may in itself indicate that the e-business hype is a phenomenon of the past). Of the papers received, eight passed a first screening by the guest editor and were subsequently made subject to a more thorough review strictly following the **mir** procedure (2–3 double-blind, peer-reviews). The review process resulted in five manuscripts accepted for publication in this special issue. All five manuscripts include empirical evidence to varying degrees. In addition to these high-quality manuscripts *I* have scrupulously utilised my guest editor privilege and included a conceptual paper of my own co-authored with *Lawrence Welch*. In this paper we aim to give an overview of the effects of the I&CT advances – and the Internet in particular – on firms' internationalisation capacities and patterns. By a firm's internationalisation *capacity* we refer to the impetus and capability of the firm to undertake international business operations, and by a firm's internationalisation *pattern* we allude to the what?, where?, when?, and how? questions of internationalisation. The paper does not attempt to be a state-of-the-art of I&CT advances and international management, however, it is meant to be an "extended introduction" to the topic – with references to the other papers of the special issue.

In the second article of the special issue *Rajesh Chakrabarti* and *Barry Scholnick* provide an empirical test of one of the suppositions that followed the proliferation of Internet users, namely "the law of one price". "The law of one price" constitutes a key element of the assumed "frictionless cyberspace" approximating the perfect, transparent market place. The authors use an impressive data base on online book prices in USA and Canada to test "the law of one price".

The article by *Thomas Lawton* and *Steven McGuire* explores the developing regulatory regime for e-commerce. The authors examine firm-government interactions in both the US and the EU to establish whether companies succeed in getting their regulatory preferences adopted. In order to determine this the authors have conducted a large number of interviews with key informants of private sector groups and high-level representatives from business, government, international organisations and NGOs.

Steven Globerman in his article sets out a conceptual model that describes how separate geographical markets might change as "global portal markets" emerge as an Internet phenomenon. The author then discuss the inferences of his conceptual model in relation to the securities market including regional and national stock exchanges. Although the Internet technology enables global "gateways" and portals challenging local markets, institutional factors obviously provides a certain conservation of the existing market separation.

Denice E. Welch, *Verner Worm*, and *Marilyn Fenwick* in their article focus on a human resource management aspect of the Internet use, namely virtual assignments. The authors examine the virtual assignments as an alternative to traditional international staffing. Their empirical point of departure is PricewaterhouseCoopers' periodic surveys of international firms operating in Europe which show a growing use of virtual assignments. The authors supplement the survey findings

Editorial

with Australian and Danish evidence of expert informants and HR managers, respectively. The Australian study, including five expert informants, uses a Delphi-type research design. In addition to eleven in-depth interviews with HR managers the Danish study reports the findings of a survey of 141 potential expatriates, as well as a pilot study of an IT multinational subsidiary.

In the last article, *Volker Mahnke* and *Markus Venzin* develop a number of thought-provoking propositions as to how digital information good characteristics may modify and extend existing internationalisation theory. An explorative, yet very comprehensive study of the high-profile, dot-com company, *eBay's*, internationalisation process serves to illustrate the need for theory development.

Taken together, the studies reported in the special issue – although of different nature in terms of research methods and questions addressed – indicate that spatial, national, and cultural factors very much determine the way companies are using the Internet in international business operations. This is the view shared by the authors and expressed in the conclusions of the articles. However, the studies also indicate that the Internet unambiguously contributes to the expansion of geographic markets relevant to the individual firm. In addition, we might expect the Internet technology to surprise us with new, unforeseen international business applications in the years to come.

I am very grateful to those colleagues who were prepared to invest time and effort to review the papers submitted to this special issue. Their contribution has been a vital necessity of this mir issue. The reviewers were (in alphabetical order): Otto Andersen, Agder University College (Norway), Svante Andersson, Halmstad University (Sweden), Ulf Andersson, Uppsala University (Sweden), Jim Bell, University of Ulster (UK), Sylvie Chetty, Massey University (New Zealand), Jerome Davies, Roskilde University (Denmark), Henrik Glimstadt, Stockholm School of Economics (Sweden), Gary Knight, Florida State University (USA), Jette Steen Knudsen, Centre for European Policy Studies (Belgium), Peter Liesch, University of Queensland (Australia), Kim Oestergaard, University of California, Berkley (USA), Murali Patibandla, Copenhagen Business School (Denmark), Rebecca Marchan Pikkari, Swedish School of Economics (Finland), Marja Tahvanainen, Helsinki School of Economics and Business Administration (Finland), Jan-Erik Vahlne, Göteborg University (Sweden), and Clas Wihlborg, Copenhagen Business School (Denmark).

Also, I would like to thank Rudolf Hastenteufel from **mir**'s Editorial Office for his expedite and careful preparation of the manuscripts in order to make them camera-ready.

Finally, I want to acknowledge Assistant Editor of **mir**, Michael-J. Oesterle, for taking initiative to this special issue, and I thank him for his never-failing enthusiasm and support during the time of preparation for this special issue.

BENT PETERSEN

mir *Edition*

Jan Hendrik Fisch

Structure Follows Knowledge

International Distribution of Research and Development in Multinational Corporations

2001, XXII, 247 pages, Br., € 49,00 (approx. US $ 45.–)
ISBN 3-409-11802-0

While the general factors influencing the internationalization of research and development are well-known, there exists neither an embracing approach to explain the international distribution of R&D activities nor one to design it efficiently.

The author develops a new model of the R&D subsystem of multinational corporations. Using modern quantitative methods the model determines both the optimal distribution of R&D activities among countries and the optimal assignment of tasks. The empirical test of the model suggests that at present not all multinational corporations show an efficient internationalization of their R&D activities.

The book addresses lecturers and students of international management, innovation management and organization theory as well as scientists and axecutives in R&D management and organizational planing.

Betriebswirtschaftlicher Verlag Dr. Th. Gabler GmbH, Abraham-Lincoln-Str. 46, 65189 Wiesbaden

Bent Petersen/Lawrence S. Welch

International Business Development and the Internet, Post-hype

Abstract

- In this paper we examine a range of effects of the Internet on international business development following the collapse of speculation and hype surrounding the 'Internet bubble' in the recent past.

- Internet effects are considered by focusing on different dimensions of firms' internationalisation: specifically, internationalisation capacity, as represented by strategy, structure, technology, human resources and financial resources; and internationalisation patterns.

Key Results

- While the Internet may have been over-hyped during the recent 'bubble' stage, there is little doubt that it has affected many aspects of companies' international operations – accelerating some stages of development, although it would appear that firms are still learning how to productively incorporate the power of the Internet across the full range of their international operations in different markets, and develop a better fit with traditional forms of operation.

Authors

Bent Petersen, Associate Professor of International Business, Department of International Economics and Management, Copenhagen Business School, Copenhagen, Denmark.
Lawrence S. Welch, Professor of International Marketing, Mt Eliza Business School, Melbourne, and University of Queensland, Brisbane, Australia.

Bent Petersen/Lawrence S. Welch

Introduction

At the beginning of the new millennium developments in the use and spread of different applications of the Internet in international business were seen by many as heralding a new era of business in which distance barriers would be removed (Economist 1995, Mol/Koppius 1999). Even the term 'international' was seen as taking on a new meaning in a 'borderless market space'. Clearly, reality has not matched the hype, and with the crash of many Internet/e-commerce related businesses it is an appropriate point to reassess where the Internet 'revolution' has taken international business so far and the implications for future development.

There is no doubt that the Internet – constituting an easy-to-access, worldwide network – has already had a significant effect on the conduct of international business and that this impact, despite the recent downturn in Internet-related businesses, is likely to continue, changing many aspects of international business in the future, although not necessarily in ways, and at the speed, that might have been expected looking ahead from the middle of the boom. Even in the boom, it was becoming clear that international expansion through the Internet posed many problems that did not have simple 'virtual solutions': for example, distributor relations could be seriously impaired by moves to bypass distributors in favour of direct dealing via the Internet; and Internet-based international retailers were already facing difficulties in expanding operations without establishing an old-style presence in foreign markets (Petersen et al. 2002).

In this article we overview major effects of the Internet on firms' internationalisation – not only those effects that are generally recognised, but also unresolved key issues. Taken together, the unresolved issues identified make up a research agenda for the study of international business development in the digital age of the 21st century. The electronic linking together of individuals, institutions, and companies in a worldwide web has created an unprecedented public data base that heralds the ultimate realisation of the information society. In this perspective, the worldwide spread of Internet use is much more than an incremental advance of information and communication technology (hereafter I & CT). Hence, when reviewing the effect of the Internet on international business development we seek to separate, on the one hand, the pervasive effects of the advances within I & CT in general, including digitisation, and, on the other hand, the *specific* effects of the Internet, including e-commerce. Furthermore, we focus on the external communication attributes of the Internet – the globally ubiquitous point-and-click interfaces based on open standards – rather than on the internal (intra-firm) communication network properties.

Our overview includes a range of impacts of the Internet on the way in which international business is evolving. We focus on firms' internationalisation, with reference to aspects such as patterns of internationalisation, mode effects, distributor relations and the role of language. We consider the effect of the Internet on the digitisation of products, and thereby the way in which companies may be able to develop international operations, and the importance of intellectual property right regimes for patterns of international expansion. In addition, we examine a number of management issues associated with increasing use of the Internet, including the management of people in a multinational context. Figure 1 presents a framework which we have employed in considering the various impacts of the Internet – adapted from Welch and Luostarinen (1988).

The figure presents two sides of a firm's internationalisation: its internationalisation *pattern* and its internationalisation *capacity*. A firm's internationalisation *pattern* refers to the different dimensions of the activities performed outside

Figure 1. Various Dimensions of Firms' Internationalisation (Adapted from Welch and Luostarinen 1988)

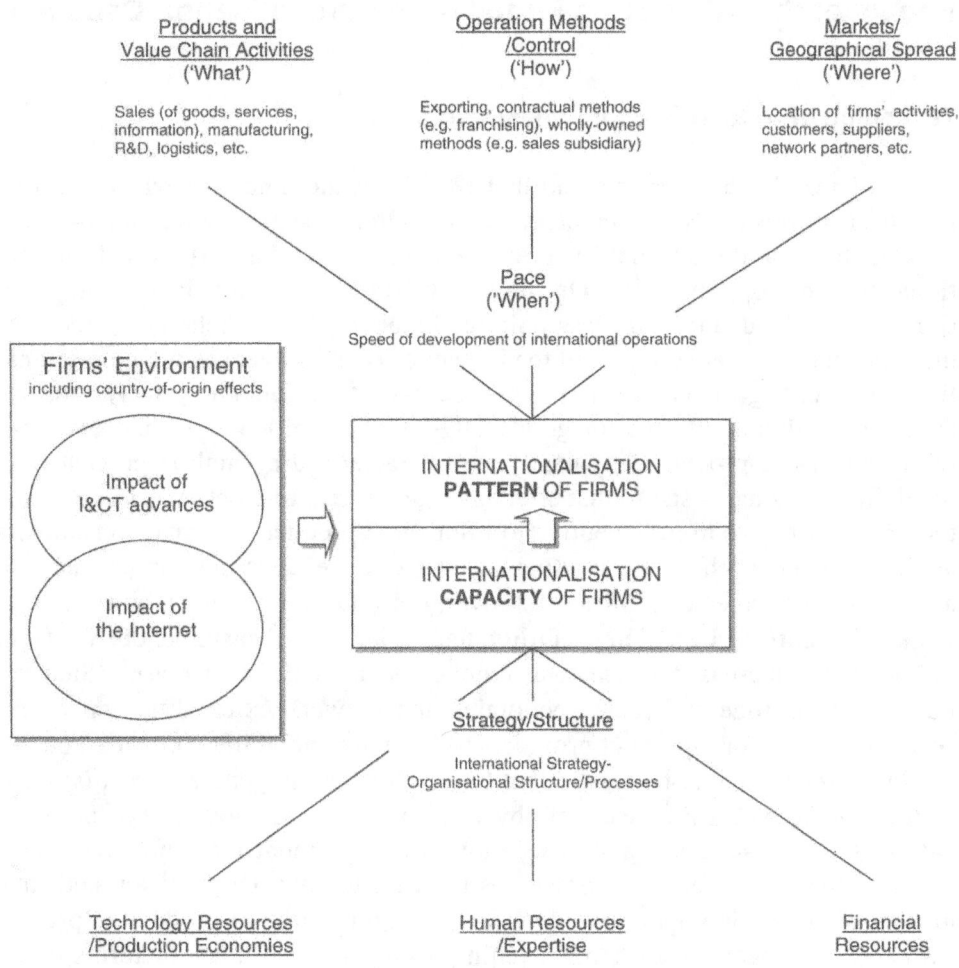

the home country – the What? How? Where? and When? questions. The internationalisation *capacity* of a firm refers to a company's's prerequisites for involving itself successfully in (further) international activities and the motivation of the company's decision makers to operate internationally. At a basic level a firm's internationalisation capacity is shown as being composed of its resource base (technological, human, and financial) that is a requisite for successful completion of international business ventures. In addition, the internationalisation strategy and organisational structure and processes of the firm are considered to be part of a firm's internationalisation capacity. Our overview of I&CT and Internet effects begins with an examination of their impact on firms' internationalisation capacity.

Impact of the Internet on Firms' Internationalisation Capacity

Technology/Production EconomiesResources

On the demand side, it is apparent that I&CT advances have provided a strong impetus for firms to become involved in international business operations – along with the fact that the Internet has greatly enhanced firms' ability to spot international business opportunities. On the supply side, internationalisation implications of I&CT advances are less unidirectional. As far as technology and production economies are concerned the impact of I&CT advances on internationalisation differs significantly between producers of 'traditional' physical goods and producers of digital information goods. Digital information goods (henceforward referred to as "e-products") typically are characterised by high fixed costs and negligible marginal costs, so that after having incurred up-front investment costs, the producer has a strong incentive to offer the e-product to as many customers as possible. Thus, the cost structure of e-products encourages the producer to achieve global scale economies. Moreover, e-products often are subject to "network externalities", by which the utility that the individual customer derives from the e-product increases as the total number of other users increases (Shapiro/ Varian 1999). Together, scale economies and network externalities provide a strong incentive for e-product providers to expand beyond the home market.

In contrast, it could be argued that I&CT advances in general have *diminished* the motivation for producers of physical/non-digitised goods to expand internationally. Because of information technology development, many producers have digitised their manufacturing processes in order to enhance precision and save manual work. As an important side-effect, the digitisation of production processes has also reduced the costs of switching from one line of manufacturing to another, thereby enabling more flexible production with a lower minimum efficient scale of operations (Westbrook/Williamson 1993, Halliburton/Jones 1994). Furthermore, I&CT investment has increased costs, relative to output, have gone down dramatically over the past two decades. individual industry, production unit costs have declined accordingly. Both of these I&CT effects have pulled in the direction of making small-scale production more economical. All else being equal, better economic conditions for small-scale production reduce firms' incentive to involve themselves in international business operations because the probability has increased that demand in the home market will exceed the minimum efficient scale of local production. Also, with more flexible production the risk of excess production capacity diminishes. Excess production capacity is considered to be an important motive for export involvement (Albaum et al. 2001). Hence, I&CT advances in terms of digitisation would appear to have reduced the pressure on producers of physical goods to go international due to production economies.

To sum up: via its influence on production economies, digitisation of *production processes* tends to decrease some firms' motivation to internationalise, whereas the digitisation of *products* is likely to increase firms' inclination to go international. However, the distinction between providers of physical goods and e-products is blurred. Today, few firms are purely physical good providers inasmuch as auxiliary services are attached to most goods, and in recent times many of these services have to a large extent been digitised (e.g. after-sales services offered through the producer's website). As this digitisation of services proceeds, firms' incentive to internationalise should grow correspondingly.

If we look at how the Internet affects the interplay between firms' production economies and internationalisation economies of scope, rather than of scale, the Internet has enhanced the possibilities of finding potential foreign partners in possession of complementary assets with which a firm may share production facilities and technology. One may suspect the realisation of scope economies via the Internet to be more important to small and medium-sized firms than to large, multinational firms. The proliferation of portals on the Internet provides evidence about firms' sharing of (scarce) resources – enabling the incumbent portal firms to serve the needs of the individual customer in a more comprehensive way than individual entities can do single-handedly.

Apparently, digitisation of goods and services together with the improved inter-firm communication opportunities offered by the Internet have changed production economies in ways that give firms a strong impetus to internationalise. One may conclude that I&CT advances, including the Internet, have improved the internationalisation capacity of firms in terms of technology and production resources. However, the increased incentive to internationalise is common to all firms in an industry across countries (although in some industries country-specific differences in level of IT infrastructure sophistication may be substantial). With more firms catering to customers outside their home market international competition inevitably becomes stronger. intensive. The crucial question for a firm's management, therefore, is to what extent improved production economies via internationalisation are matched by international competitors pursuing similar scale and scope economies? extended into foreign markets? The Internet appears to be an excellent instrument for gauging a firm's competitive advantage in an international setting. With its outstanding search capabilities, the Internet may assist the individual firm in benchmarking itself against its international competitors. On the other hand, strategic information about technology, or other sources of competitive advantage, is not readily available on the Internet. Hence, whereas the Internet undoubtedly is an excellent mediator of information about demand side conditions in international markets, it is an unresolved issue as to what extent the Internet is of use when it comes to supply side information.

Human Resources – Managing People

The Internet has had important effects on the way in which people are managed within international companies. How the process is handled may well have profound implications for the capacity of companies to internationalise and handle its outcomes. The ability of companies to develop global operations increasingly via the Internet depends on staff being able to initiate and carry through a range of new activities and deal with a variety of new technologies. This will place major demands on the human resources function to find the appropriate staff, either inside or outside the organisation. A range of new skills has to be developed, not the least being, for some, to operate in a cross cultural environment without the normal person-to-person exchanges (Petersen et al. 2002). This is probably the most demanding aspect of global e-commerce, although the emergence of international call centres has demonstrated that staff can be trained to undertake a range of functions, and communicate with customers in a variety of languages, and even dialects, in a relatively impersonal international environment. The rapid growth of call centres and document processing facilities in India has demonstrated something of the possibilities in this area (Economist 2001). Moves in this direction, however, make it somewhat more difficult for management to decide when it may be necessary to move between e-servicing and more traditional forms of customer servicing. In establishing centralised e-response systems, companies can create barriers to the holistic, seamless servicing of customers (Widdows/Widdows 1999). Particularly in cross-cultural situations, companies will often have to develop person-to-person encounters with foreign customers at an early stage in the process of foreign market entry. The link between e-servicing and more personalised approaches to foreign customers, therefore, may depend on some individuals who can move easily between these different forms of customer servicing. Again, the demand on higher levels of training and skills may be considerable, as well as greater flexibility on the part of staff. It would seem that companies using the Internet in the international arena are only just coming to terms with the demands and possibilities of the new Internet-driven environment for staffing and training issues.

While the Internet itself is likely to alleviate some of these demands, such as via e-learning, it cannot be viewed as a 'cure-all' in international operations. Recent research in Denmark (see article by Welch, Worm and Fenwick in this issue) illustrates this in respect to the growth of so-called virtual assignments (i.e. managing a foreign staff activity via the Internet rather than in-person). Their use has been supplemented by a rise in short term assignments. Ultimately, there would appear to be some scope for a reduction in the need for staff movement internationally. I&CT advances have already improved conditions for expatriation and short term assignments by making it much easier for the expatriate and his/her family to keep in contact with their networks back home. With the Internet, however, conditions for virtual assignments have improved significantly as well. The interest in virtual teams and virtual assignments reflects an effort on the part of many companies to derive benefits from Internet technology in the way they organise and manage staff activities within their international operations (Kayworth/Leidner 2000). Foreign assignments, no matter how short they are, represent a costly side of international firms' operations, and therefore a continuing incentive for the search for alternatives (Dowling et al. 1999).

Financial Resources

I&CT advances in general have been important drivers of the convergence of costs of capital of firms during the last decade (Oxelheim 1997, see the article by Globerman in this issue). As a result of this process of transition from independent national financial markets to a more integrated, globalised market international firms have, all else being equal, lost competitive advantage vis-à-vis domestic firms operating in what previously may have been high-cost capital markets. Since the availability of cheap and abundant (venture) capital in global markets currently appears to be declining, of drying out f firms' incentive to internationalise should diminish accordingly. However, through the creation of more transparency across markets, I&CT advances, and the Internet in particular, may reduce the disadvantage of foreignness in terms of being unknown to local investors.

Assuming that the Internet has the effect of increasing the pace of internationalisation – for example, opening up a wider range of foreign markets that can be served – the ability to finance expansion may become a critical issue, particularly for new Internet-related ventures in the post "Internet bubble" world. A study of a small number of internationalising, Internet-based Norwegian firms indicated that while it was relatively easy to obtain finance (via investors) to support international expansion in the Internet-positive environment of the late-1990s, this has become much tougher today, leading to cutbacks in international commitments (Borsheim/Solberg 2002). The Internet should facilitate greater transparency about financing options on an international basis, thereby adding to pressure for lowering the cost of capital across countries. This could be an important consideration for Internet-related new ventures given the variability of markets for new venture finance.

International Strategy/Organisational Structure and Processes

Whereas I&CT advances have supported firms' strategies of multinationality and transnationality (Bartlett/Ghoshal 2000), the advent of the Internet seems to have placed pressure on international companies for increased global integration and coordination (Roche 2000). The expectation at the height of the Internet boom was that international companies would experience a stronger need for global standardisation as a result of increased transparency across national markets (Roche 2000). This, in turn, would force international firms toward stronger central coordination and control mechanisms, involving closer integration of their dispersed activities. As an example of Internet-induced transparency, pricing policies in different national markets would need to be brought more closely into line (Roche 2000). Inevitably, such a change would force a whole range of adjustments throughout the international company in areas such as purchasing, supply chain management, and marketing programmes. As a reflection of this move towards centralisation, some international companies introduced websites for the corporation as a whole, and for international operating companies in non-English speaking countries, such as Denmark, the website would normally be in English. The centralisation bias of the Internet has been reinforced by the perceived strategic importance of online sales by international companies so that the direction and control of developments have been driven by headquarters – it has been seen as being too important to leave to the various subsidiaries. This has been applied in particular to testing in the marketplace of online sales of existing as well as new products (Confederation of Danish Industries, forthcoming). It is somewhat ironic that in the digital age there seems to be something of a return of the product life cycle pattern stressed in earlier development of international business patterns (Burenstam-Linder 1961, Vernon 1966).

However, the extent to which the Internet has changed markets in the direction of becoming more transparent and price competitive is open to question (see the article by Chakrabati/Scholnick in this issue). There are undoubtedly areas where this has occurred (Yip 2000), and the processes are continuing, but in reality companies have been able to maintain strategies of differentiation in many areas of business across global markets. In part they have been able to do this because of increasing skills in utilising the Internet to strengthen supplier and customer relations in a way that adds value to the product offer. The increasing use by companies of the Internet as a platform for extranets that more effectively link companies to suppliers and customers has been an important element of this evolving process. Furthermore, the website has become another element of this process, allowing companies to separate and inform suppliers and customers as part of building longer term relations. In an Australian study of the use of e-commerce by SMEs, a number of companies were found to have reached the stage of integration with their trading partners via the web site, linking internal business systems and processes (Marshall/McKay 2002). This becomes even more important in various foreign markets because of language and cultural differences. Finally, the marketplace of tomorrow may very well witness pressure for increased local responsiveness enabled by I&CT, an element of the move to "mass customisation" heralded by some marketers (Halliburton/Jones 1994, Westbrook/Williamson 1993), and fuelled by anti-globalisation sentiments among consumers. Local responsiveness will not necessarily comply with national borders,

Table 1. Major Effects of I&CT Advances and Internet on Firms' Internationalisation Capacity

INTERNATIO-NALISATION CAPACITY OF FIRMS	General I&CT advancement effect(s)	Specific Internet effect	Unresolved Internet key issues
Technology Resources/ Production Economies	• Product digitisation encourages internationalisation of firms • Process digitisation reduces need for internationalisation	Improved conditions for sharing of production facilities and technology resources between firms	Does the Internet ease firms' assessment of their competitive advantage in foreign markets?
Human Resources/ Expertise	Improved conditions for expatriation and short term assignments	Improved conditions for virtual assignments	Exacerbation of culture/language-related conflicts within the international organisation?
Financial Resources	Global convergence of cost of capital of international firms	First abundant, then scarce, national capital available to international e-commerce ventures	Does greater transparency give easier access to foreign capital for int'l e-commerce ventures?
International Strategy/Organisational Structure and Processes	Enabling multinationality and trans-nationality	Pressure for increased global coordination	• Pressure for increased local responsiveness? • Centralisation via e-business hegemony of HQ?

but may appear as a super-segmentation phenomenon where the individual customer requires special treatment.

Despite the many claims of the changed world in the digital age, it would appear that many of the 'old' management issues remain: companies still have to balance the conflicting pressures of local responsiveness while maintaining managerial oversight, control and coordination from headquarters.

So far, we have discussed a range of impacts of the Internet and e-commerce developments on the internationalisation of companies – as reflected in their internationalisation capacity (see lower part of Figure 1). Some of the main effects are summarised in Table 1. As well, though, there are important effects of the Internet on the way firms carry out international business operations (reflected in their internationalisation patterns – see Figure 1, upper part), and it is to these impacts we shall now turn.

The Impact of the Internet on Firms' Internationalisation Patterns

Pace

As yet, there has been limited research on the impact of the Internet on the internationalisation of firms, particularly of a longitudinal nature. Nevertheless, it seems evident that the Internet has enabled much faster internationalisation to occur for some firms, and the speeding up of processes at certain stages for other companies (Lituchy/Rail 2000, Vahlne/Johanson 2002). The accelerated internationalisation induced by the Internet is mainly due to demand side effects: companies are pulled into foreign markets via their greater visibility to customers using the Internet to search for products and services. Thereby, the Internet effect on the pace of firms' internationalisation differs from the general effect of I&CT advances that have been more supply side oriented. For example, as a result of I&CT advances, the lead time of technology development has shortened, which in turn has tended to result in international companies accelerating their penetration of foreign markets.

Depending on the type of product or service, some companies have been able to achieve global spread in a relatively short space of time by operating solely via the Internet, e.g. dot.com. companies and Internet consulting companies (Economist 1995, Vahlne/Johanson 2002). As well, the Internet has facilitated processes such as international information searches, exchange of information, and through the web site the potential means of relatively instantaneous contact with the rest of the world. It can be argued that the Internet has 'reversed' the constraint posed by lack of information/knowledge about foreign markets shown in widespread research on exporting firms to being one of pulling firms into international markets (Leonidou/Katsikeas 1997, McAuley 1993, Seringhaus 1986). In a review of the research on export barriers, Leonidou (1995, p. 40) concluded that "limited information to locate/analyze foreign markets had the greatest inhibiting impact on the firm's ability to initiate or develop exports".

The Internet probably has ensured that the "born global" (or international new venture) phenomenon (Knight/Cavusgil 1996, Madsen/Servais 1997) is a more commonplace reality in the process of firms' internationalisation – increasing the likelihood of fortuitous international Internet contact and unsolicited contact via a company's web site whether international sales were an objective or not (Quelch/Klein 1996, Yip 2000). This process has undoubtedly been reinforced by the actions of different countries' trade promotion bodies which have become active in using the Internet in various ways to enhance the potential of local companies to connect with potential foreign customers. An example is a recent initiative by the Japan External Trade Organization (JETRO) in which Japanese IT companies interested in doing business with Australian IT firms were introduced to potential Australian clients via the Internet (JETRO 2002).

While the Internet is likely to positively affect the rate of firms' internationalisation, the effect is by no means certain: much depends on the interplay between culture and the greater rate at which people are contacting each other via the Internet. It is conceivable that greater contact could be a cross-cultural negative, i.e. the Internet may well connect people prematurely, without the preceding development of cross-cultural familiarisation. Leamer and Storper (2001) argue from the perspective of economic geography that increasing economic development has placed even greater stress on the transmission of complex messages and data through face-to-face contacts that the Internet can never replace.

Product/Value Chain Activity

The potential of the Internet for trading purely e-products has spawned a new array of digitised products.

As shown in Figure 2, many of these products are aimed at servicing the use of the Internet and facilitating e-commerce activity – especially different types of software connected with payments, security systems, customer profiling, etc. The Internet has also stimulated new developments in the field of machine translation as different languages are used on web sites and through the Internet (Economist 2002). As well, many "old products" are becoming digitised, thereby allowing them to be sold and transferred through the Internet; for example, the emergence of so-called e-books. Such books are being sold by publishers alongside Internet sales of physical books (e.g. by Amazon) and the continuing use of retailers sel-

Figure 2. The Internet, I&CT Development, and Internationalisation

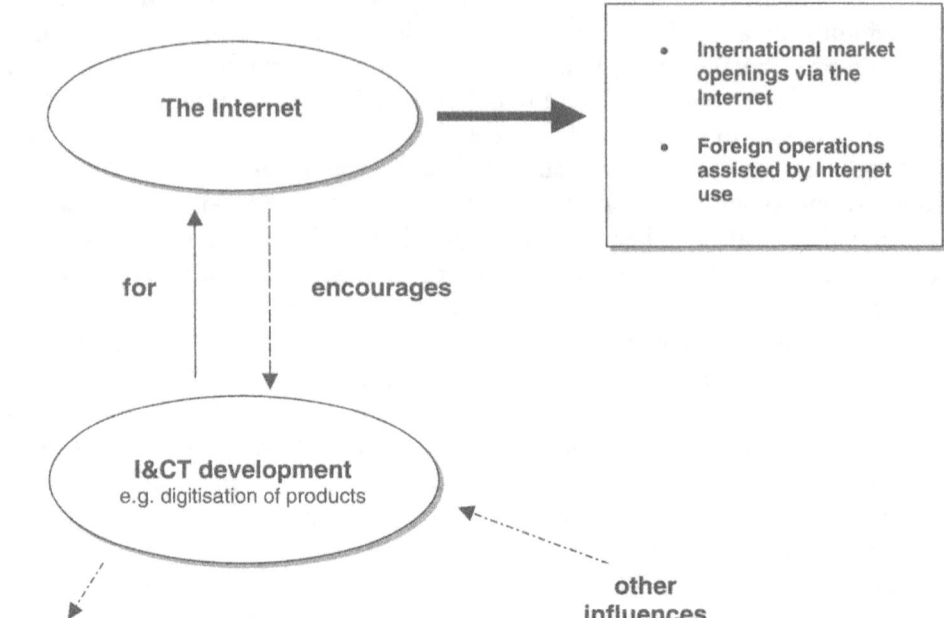

ling directly to the public. There has been, similarly, an expanded range of 'entertainment' products that have been digitised and offered via the Internet, such as films and music, that co-exist with traditional forms of delivery. Of course, companies will often be selling a mix or combination of purely e-products and those of a traditional, physical kind. The digitisation of products in combination with the Internet as an inter-firm collaboration facilitator (e.g. as manifested by the appearance of Internet portals) has also been seen as an opportunity for firms to provide more comprehensive product solutions to their customers (Gupta 2002).

In addition to a possible digitisation/Internet-induced shift from discrete products to comprehensive customer solutions, digitisation holds the potential for changing the focus of firms' overseas value added activities. The digitisation of products first of all has implications for the market-seeking value chain activities that firms undertake abroad: other things being equal, digitisation should mean less need for localisation of marketing and sales activities abroad (later, we will discuss the validity of this argument). Other value chain activities, such as research and development, are less amenable to digitisation because personal networks and tacit knowledge are important components, and resource seeking activities (raw material extraction, exploitation of cheap labour, etc.) are even less affected by digitisation.

Some services (e.g. car repairs) are bound to remain physically oriented, but others may be shifted to delivery over the Internet. To the extent that after-sales service can be handled via the Internet, companies will feel less pressure to set up on the ground servicing arrangements in foreign markets, and may be able to avoid foreign direct investment in some cases. Yip (2000, p.12) maintains that "many companies now handle much of their global after-sales service through their websites. Cisco, for example, provides 80% of its service over the web". In much the same way as systems sales typically involve a combination of goods, services and know-how, increasingly complex combinations of e- and non e-products and services can be expected to develop. Expanded e-product and service offerings and their utilisation are bound to increase in the near future as mobile telephones increasingly come into play as an alternative, even preferred, means to receive Internet-based products and services.

Clearly, much of the digitisation of products and services is driven by a range of influences, not only those tied to Internet use, as shown in Figure 2. However, the Internet is an important driver in this process. Likewise, the possibility of translating such product development into an expansion of options for global e-commerce expansion is an important factor. Developments noted above can be seen as facilitating other aspects of companies' internationalisation: e.g., the pace of internationalisation, the spread of markets served and the ability to avoid a shift to more traditional forms of foreign operations. At the same time though, intellectual property rights (IPR) regimes and associated legal problems have tended to act as a constraining influence on the facilitating benefits of digitisation, affecting product development in two important ways: (1) constraining the development and international marketing of e-products which are difficult to protect; (2) biasing the development process towards products which will enhance security on the Internet and IPR protection. We will return to these IPR aspects when discussing firms' selection of foreign markets.

While early internationalisation processes may be facilitated by the Internet, sporadic evidence indicates that even purely Internet-based firms find it difficult to operate internationally without establishing local, physical facilities, e.g. representative offices, at some stage, thereby slowing internationalisation at a later stage. The Danish dot.com company, Speednames (a wholly-owned subsidiary of Ascio Technologies Inc.), provides an example of how difficult it may be – even for companies selling purely digitised products – to reach customers outside the home market. Since its inception in 1999, Speednames has offered worldwide sales of Internet domain names as a digital domain name registrar. Speednames operates as an intermediary between the local domain name authority, called Registry, and individuals or business organisations that want a domain name. Global identity is of strategic importance to the company: it has deliberately disguised its national (Danish) identity. The website (www.speednames.com) gives information in nine different languages. As part of its international marketing, Speednames appears on all important Internet search engines in order to be visible to customers looking for domain name providers. Despite all of these online marketing efforts, a customer survey (Summer 2001) showed that more than 50% of Speednames' customers were domiciled in Denmark. The bigger markets of the USA (6% of Speednames' customers), Sweden (6%), the UK (5%), Germany (3%) and the Netherlands (3%) contributed relatively few customers. Speednames' low penetration of the international market points to the importance of conventional — and very localised – communication channels (word-of-mouth, exposure in Danish business magazines, etc.) rather than online promotion. Recognising the limits of online promotion as a stand-alone marketing tool, by Spring 2002 the management of Speednames had considered using new, supplementary operation modes — such as franchising and sales agencies – in its more important foreign markets (personal communication with Product Manager, Christine Agger-Nielsen and Managing Director, J. Helbrandt).

The case of Speednames is in line with the findings of a recent study of Internet users in twenty countries (Lynch/Beck 2001). The study indicated that being online was not enough to produce global operations. Customers still looked for localisation (context/culture) in their online experience. Similarly, in a study of a small number of Norwegian born global, Internet-based firms, it was found that even when direct exporting via the Internet was used, it was quickly followed by other forms of operation in the foreign market (Borsheim/Solberg 2002).

For those firms producing physical products for export, the perceived need to localise will sometimes come quite early as a result of the complexities of physical distribution, e.g. for foreign wine companies in coping with diverse State laws regarding the sale of alcohol in the US. In whatever form foreign operations occur after Internet driven sales have taken place, firms will have to confront a range of new demands and commitments that will inevitably slow down the rate of internationalisation. It is unclear how much of the learning and network development that occurs through Internet-based internationalisation can be adapted to non-Internet-based operations. The new operations are likely to require a range of new learning tasks, including the role of the Internet in combination with more traditional operation forms (Petersen et al. 2002).

Foreign Operation Mode Effects

Having recognised the need for a local, physical presence in the foreign market, companies have to decide whether such operations should be internalised or not (Buckley/Casson 1976). The general view is that I&CT advances favour externalisation because the possibilities for enforcing contracts entered into with local operators are enhanced (Blaine/Bowen 2000). The opportunities for the contract partner to shirk would be mitigated by online monitoring, access to data bases, integration of accounting systems and the like, of the contractual partners (Marshall/McKay 2002). As an example, some franchisors have been able to achieve very close monitoring of their franchisees' operations including sales data, ordering systems, customer behaviour (data mining), etc. through the use of on-line linkages and software. In addition, I&CT advances have reduced not only the costs of enforcing market contracts (market transaction costs), but also the costs of coordinating the activities of the multinational company. With a simultaneous reduction of transaction and coordination costs, the net effect of I&CT advances in terms of foreign operation modes is difficult to predict. In a similar vein to Internet effects, at the outset the Internet was predicted to accentuate the externalisation effect of I&CT advances because companies, through the Internet, would experience better opportunities for detecting suitable contractual partners, such as franchisees, in foreign markets. As a result, the Internet could be expected to provide a fillip to franchising's development internationally. Franchising companies in many cases are seeking to build a global concept for which the Internet is well-suited (Yip 2000). The Internet is suited also to publicising and promoting opportunities to potential franchisees and in generating approaches from them. The Internet should also allow the franchisor to be more responsive to franchisees and their customers – adding value to the customer offer in a way that could dramatically change the balance between franchisor and franchisee, especially when this is put alongside the enhanced monitoring capabilities via I&CT advances, including the Internet. As a result, franchisors may look for increased returns from franchisees.

However, the pressure for global coordination mentioned earlier may force international companies into internalisation simply because a very high control of the international affiliate network is required. Hence, it is difficult to establish whether or not I&CT advances and the Internet promote contractual modes rather than internalisation. Furthermore, empirical evidence of a trend towards more use of contractual forms in international operations is problematic inasmuch as there may be substantial time lags in relation to change of existing organisational forms, and because an externalisation effect may 'drown' in countervailing effects, such as information overload and an increasing importance of tacit knowledge as a competitive advantage factor (Daft/Lengel 1986, Blaine/Bowen 2000, Leamer et al. 2001).

Whereas it is difficult to predict I&CT/Internet effects in terms of externalisation/internalisation it is less disputable that the Internet – in combination with digitisation – will result in expanded exporting activity. If the technology allows companies to operate on a purely electronic basis, or nearly so, then we can describe the 'cross-border' activity in cyberspace as a type of exporting – *Internet exporting*. Where physical goods are involved, the Internet should allow companies to operate as exporters without the same pressure to move to other forms of operation such as foreign subsidiaries. As noted above, the reality has proven somewhat different, i.e. there is still pressure to set up local, physical facilities – examples of local, *non-physical* presence of an entrant dot-com firm are a local domain site or a specialised foreign language website focused on the local market, but under a country-of-origin domain (Kotha et al. forthcoming). While the Internet can do some things well – e.g. initial contact, etc. – there is still the need to relate to customers in a more direct way in their own environment. Internet exporting exposes a company to competitive approaches via the same medium. An issue, then, is how to lock in foreign customers. How best to do this is still an open question for companies.

As to the Internet potential for bypassing middlemen that has been predicted (see e.g. Wunderman 1998), thereby diminishing the role of agents/distributors, this does not appear to have eventuated, certainly not at the rate which has been predicted (Coltman et al. 2001, Sarkar et al. 1998). There are numerous, often high-profile, examples of companies becoming involved in damaging conflict with their distributors/retailers in the process of attempting to develop direct online sales, e.g. Compaq in Australia, Lego in the UK, and Levi Strauss in the US. A study of 50 manufacturers found that the biggest issue facing them in selling online was channel conflict – far above any other issue (66% mentioned channel conflict) (Allen 2000). One might argue that in an international business context the difficulty of bypassing a local intermediary is even more pronounced due to cultural and communication issues. The focus of the research in this area has tended to be on the potential channel conflict between manufacturer and distributor, with an implicit assumption that the manufacturer has the upper hand with regard to the development of online operations. However, it cannot be excluded that a distributor will have developed sophisticated online outlets and associated distribution infrastructure, to the extent that the distributor has a significant advantage over the foreign firm through a combination of Internet and physical distribution activities. In fact, there is every reason for the distributor to develop in this direction as a way of warding off the inroads of the Internet into their position in the marketplace. It is conceivable that the distributor with this combination will be in a stronger position than previously.

Geographical Spread

The Internet can be expected to accelerate the rate at which certain aspects of internationalisation proceed, but also it creates the likelihood that companies will create costumers in a broader array of countries than was experienced in the past at equivalent stages of internationalisation. This is because of the global exposure consequent upon the establishment of a web site. Markets which may never have been considered feasible due to language or other cultural differences could be opened up by the Internet – often fortuitously. At a macro level, of course, the growth of market diversification options is tied to the rate at which Internet use diffuses globally. Thus, countries' technological infrastructure development, including diffusion rate of Internet users, has been found to be a major country entry choice criterion of US Internet firms (Kotha et al. forthcoming). Assuming they respond to the diverse market options presented, companies will be required to deal with a broader range of cultures than hitherto. In seeking to make their international operations profitable, they will face the question of how much market diversification they can actually handle (Ayal/Zif 1979, Piercy 1981).

The extent of spread will be affected by companies' Internet language policy. Small companies may be ill equipped to handle multiple languages via the Internet. For example, in a study of small inns and bed and breakfasts, Lituchy and Rail (2000, p.95) found that "although they are trying to increase the number of guests from other countries [via the Internet], most of the respondents [operators of the inns and bed and breakfasts] had information only in English". Even large multinationals seem to have had difficulties in developing and operating multilingual web sites (Economist 2002). Thus, language would appear to be an obvious constraint on the extent of market spread by internationalising companies through the Internet. This constraint appears to be growing with the increasing use of own language Internet services in individual countries (Welch et al. 2001).

Although in the initial stages of global expansion of the Internet English was overwhelmingly the language used in Internet communication and dominated websites, there has been a dramatic reduction in its role in recent times (Global Reach 2002). Increasingly, the Internet and websites have become a vehicle for localisation through the use of local languages, although often associated with an English option (Welch et al. 2001). This development parallels what has happened in the provision of media/entertainment services. For example, in the early stages of European growth of the sports channel, Eurosport, it was dominated by use of English language commentary. However, in the longer term it has been localising by providing commentary in the local language where it is being broadcast, facilitated by improvements in the relevant technology.

Market patterns of firms' Internet-based international expansion also are affected by the type of intellectual property rights (IPR) regime in different countries. By their very nature, digital information goods, or e-products, can be readily copied and reproduced (Shapiro/Varian 1999). The problem for those marketing these products and seeking to derive revenue from them is the difficulty of extracting payment from their use. Examples abound of companies being unable to prevent unauthorised use, and even resale of their e-products. Publishers have been struggling to make e-books a viable commercial entity. To the extent that it is difficult to protect intellectual property, this is likely to constrain the preparedness of companies to develop domestic as well as international e-operations. Very much in contrast to the inherent global nature of e-commerce, the legal systems by which intellectual property rights are overwhelmingly defined in a national or regional context.

It would seem that the issue of intellectual property rights has an effect on the internationalisation of companies in a number of ways. Companies may find that IPR regimes in some foreign countries are weaker than at home, and for this reason exclude these countries as hosting sites for production and, in particular, R&D entities. The risk of damaging use of companies' e-products may even result in attempts to restrict export sales to customers domiciled in countries with weak IPR regimes – i.e. generating what might be called a 'country-of-destination' bias. Technically, the very nature of e-products makes it impossible to prevent a local customer from passing on e-products to these 'banned' locations, with the intention of reproducing the e-products; but legally, companies can more readily take action against the local customer engaged in such activity. Many companies have sought to deal with the problem of dissemination risk by widespread patenting, where feasible, of various aspects of operating systems and software in conjunction with the use of the Internet. Perhaps the best known example is that of the computer assembler and retailer Dell which has taken out many patents on its Internet ordering system. As such, this approach has been an important part of clearing the way for the development of its international marketing operations. In this way, IPR regimes can be an important factor in the general pattern of firms' internationalisation. To some extent it can be argued that the increased importance of the legal environment in the digital age has likewise raised its profile within the psychic distance box.

The above discussion of IPR regimes, culture, language, and technology infrastructure demonstrates that the world of global e-commerce is not seamless, and that country differences in various aspects of e-commerce remain important, shaping resulting patterns of global e-commerce.

The main effects of I&CT advances and the Internet on firms' internationalisation patterns – as outlined in the four previous sections – are summarised in Table 2.

Firm's Environment

As indicated in Figure 1, the development of firms' internationalisation capacity and patterns are, of course, influenced by other environmental factors than the Internet and I&CT advances in general. Important environmental factors include exchange rate fluctuations, trade bloc developments, governmental export promotion programmes, e-commerce tax regulation, and economic growth in general. Some environmental factors are to some extent influenced by Internet development itself; take as an example the impact of e-learning on the educational level of a country's work force.

Table 2. Major Effects of I&CT Advances and Internet on Firms' Internationalisation Patterns

INTERNATIO-NALISATION PATTERNS OF FIRMS	General I&CT advancement effect(s)	Specific Internet effect(s)	Unresolved Internet key issues
Pace (When?)	Accelerated internationalisation	Accelerated internationalisation – due to demand side effects	Does the internationalisation of dot-com firms slow down in later stages?
Product/Value Chain Activity (What?)	• Digitisation of products • Shift from market seeking to resource seeking activities	• Cross-border e-commerce • Shift from discrete products to comprehensive solutions	To what extent does the Internet supersede firms' need for local, physical presence?
Operational Method/ Control (How?)	Use of contractual methods favoured by improved controllability	• Contractual methods favoured by broader recruitment base • More Internet exports	Does the pressure for global coordination (induced by the Internet) cause greater internalisation of foreign operations?
Geographical Spread (Where?)	More diversified country portfolio	More diversified country portfolio – due to demand side effects	To what extent does the Internet make geographical segmentation irrelevant?

We will restrict the discussion to one particular environmental factor, namely country-of-origin effects. This factor has direct implications for firms' export opportunities in the digital age, and may, or may not, be redefined by the Internet. Country-of-origin effects are part of this impact of country differences (Tse/Gorn 1993). Consider the difficulties of a Russian firm attempting to develop international operations through the Internet, with particular emphasis on selling e-products directly to consumers in the US market. To begin with, it is likely to face concerns regarding products and services originating in Russia (assuming this is not hidden), as with physical products. In addition, however, there are other factors further complicating these concerns. Take for example payment systems where there has been a reluctance on the part of consumers in many countries to undertake payment by credit cards because of security concerns (Oxley/Yeung 2001). The need to put credit card details into the hands of Russian companies is likely to constrain the preparedness of US consumers to become involved in Internet purchases from such companies – thus reinforcing perceived country-of-origin concerns. The establishment of a US domain website may reduce the concerns of US customers, but not eliminate them.

One solution for the Russian company would be for it to establish a US-based, physical facility in a way which would allow it to utilise a made-in-US label. This could apply to both physical and e-products. In general, there is some evidence that e-commerce and related companies are moving quite early to establish offices in countries which they are seeking to penetrate (Borsheim/Solberg 2002, Vahlne/Johanson 2002).

Conclusion and Implications

From an overview of the way in which the Internet and its many manifestations are affecting companies' continued development of international operations, one might conclude that 'the Internet hype is dead, long live the Internet'. Companies have not stopped looking at ways of more effectively using the Internet in their international activities, although the crash of the "Internet bubble" may have taken off some of the perceived pressure to push ahead rapidly. As a result, companies should be in a better position to weld together what the Internet is capable of delivering with the strength of traditional approaches – perhaps this is the most important change in approach 'post-hype'. Porter (2001) stresses the importance of linking traditional forms of doing business with on-line approaches in the development of strategy. He quotes the case of one US distributor which found that the distribution of its printed catalogue resulted in increased on-line sales. This is particularly important in an international context, where cross-cultural exchanges are a constant challenge. An illustration is the continuing difficulty that even large multinationals have in coping with a multiplicity of languages. As yet, technological solutions have provided only a limited answer, and it is evident that, in general, the power of face-to-face relations is difficult to replace, as is the role of distributors in foreign markets.

Already, it has become evident that in analysing the impact of the Internet on internationalisation there needs to be more attention paid to time and process effects. For example, it seems to be broadly accepted that the Internet will play an increasing role in initial contact between companies and their foreign customers, reinforced by various governments' Internet-related trade promotion activities, and generating more so-called 'born global' firms. However, over time it is likely that the Internet will play a more complex role in the process of foreign market servicing – interacting with other approaches such as foreign market visits, foreign intermediaries, external advertising, etc. In this respect, the Internet may actually make the position of the new entrant to international operations even more difficult. The new entrant not only has to face the reality of being an unknown amongst a voluminous world of would-be entrants, but also has to face the demands of building experience with using the Internet internationally, of developing a broader range of activities and dealing with a multiplicity of cross-cultural relations in more dispersed markets, and, in the process, link Internet use to other elements of foreign market operations: a tall order, and growing taller. As in the past, newly internationalising companies are bound to look for ways of making this process easier to handle – for example, in the choice of markets to service: psychic distance is unlikely to disappear as a factor in an Internet-influenced world. It may become even more pronounced, reinforced by intellectual property rights considerations, payment security, and related legal concerns.

While the Internet enhances many aspects of the ability of headquarters to control and direct what happens in a multinational's subsidiaries, it does not remove the need for local responsiveness, and in a perverse sense, the Internet and related technology enhance many aspects of local responsiveness – especially in building tighter, common language links to local customers and suppliers, with all the associated strengthening possibilities of face-to-face encounters, sometimes an essential prelude to effective Internet-based relationships. Companies will undoubtedly go through a variety of approaches in the course of modifying management approaches to take account of the realities and possibilities of the Internet. This is already evident in the use of staff in foreign assignments. Companies appear to be testing the limits of the possibilities of virtual assignments, although it appears that these still have to be supplemented with a range of visiting arrangements, short of full expatriation. In this, as in many other areas, as people in all countries learn how to use the Internet to more effectively carry out international business, a blending of 'old forms' of international operations with the power of the Internet is likely emerge – in contrast to the "Internet changes everything" world predicted by some.

References

Albaum, G./Strandskov, J./Duerr, E., *International Marketing and Export* Management, fourth edition, Prentice Hall 2001.
Allen, L., Channel Conflict Crumbles, *The Forrester Report*, March 2000 (www.forrester.com), pp. 1–16.
Ayal, I./Zif, J., Market Expansion Strategies in Multinational Marketing, *Journal of Marketing*, 43, 2, 1979, pp. 84–94.
Bartlett, C. A./Ghoshal, S., *Transnational Management*, third edition, Boston, MA: McGraw Hill 2000.
Benito, G. R. G./Welch, L. S., Foreign Market Servicing: Beyond Choice of Entry Mode, *Journal of International Marketing*, 2, 2, 1994, pp. 7–27.
Blaine, M. J./Bowen, J., The Role of Information Technology in International Business Research, in Roche, E. M./Blaine, M. J. (eds.), *Information Technology in Multinational Enterprises*, Cheltenham, UK: Edward Elgar 2000, pp. 21–56.

Borsheim, J. H./Solberg, C. A., *The Internationalization of Born Global Internet Firms*, Cahiers de Recherche, Bordeaux École de Management, Talence, France 2002.
Buckley, P./Casson, M., *The Future of the Multinational Enterprise*, London: Macmillan 1976.
Burenstam-Linder, S., *An Essay on Trade and Transformation*, Uppsala: Almqvist and Wiksell 1961.
Coltman, T./Devinney, T./Latukefu, A./Midgley, D. F., E-business: Revolution, Evolution, or Hype?; *California Management Review*, 44, 1, 2001, pp. 57–86.
Confederation of Danish Industries, *E-Business and International Marketing Profiles of Danish Firms* [Danish title: E-business og danske virksomheders internationale afsætningsprofil], Copenhagen, forthcoming.
Cross, R./Borgatti, S. P./Parker, A., Making Invisible Work Visible: Using Social Network Analysis to Support Strategic Collaboration, *California Management Review*, 44, 2, 2002, pp. 25–46.
Daft, R. L./Lengel, R. H., Organizational Information Requirements, Media Richness and Structural Design, *Management Science*, 32, 5, 1986, pp. 554–571.
Dowling P. J./Welch D. E./Schuler R. S., *International Human Resource Management: Managin People in a Multinational Context*, 3rd edition, Cincinatti, OH: South-Western College 1999.
Economist, The Death of Distance, September 30, 1995, Special Section, pp. 5–7.
Economist, Outsourcing to India, May 5, 2001, pp.61–63.
Economist, Tongues of the Web, *Technology Quarterly*, March 16, 2002, pp. 20–22.
Global Reach, *Website:* http://www.glreach.com/globstats/
Gupta, A. K., The Multinational Enterprise in the Digital Age, *Presentation* at the AIB Annual Meeting, San José, Puerto Rico, June 28–July 1, 2002.
Halliburton, C./Jones, I., Global Individualism – Reconciling Global Marketing and Global Manufacturing, *Journal of International Marketing*, 2, 4, 1994, pp. 79–88.
Japan External Trade Organization, JETRO Launches "Virtual IT Mission to Australia", JETRO press release, February 20, 2002.
Kayworth, T./Leidner, D., The Global Virtual Manager: A Prescription for Success, *European Management Journal*, 18, 2, 2000, pp. 183–194.
Knight, G./Cavusgil, S. T., The Born Global Firm: A Challenge to Traditional Internationalization Theory, *Advances in International Marketing*, 8, 1996., pp. 11–26.
Kotha, S./Rothaermel, F. T./Steensma, K., Technological Sophistication versus Cultural Similarity: An Empirical Analysis of Country Factors Influencing Location Decisions in the Internationalization of Internet Firms, *Strategic Management Journal*, forthcoming.
Leamer, E. E./Storper, M., The Economic Geography of the Internet Age, *Journal of International Business Studies*, 32, 4, 2001, pp. 641–666.
Leonidou, L. C., Empirical Research on Export Barriers: Review, Assessment and Synthesis, *Journal of International Marketing*, 3, 1, 1995, pp. 29–43.
Leonidou, L. C./Katsikeas, C. S., Export Information Sources: The Role of Organizational and Internationalization Influences, *Journal of Strategic Marketing*, 5, 1997, pp. 65–87.
Lituchy, T.R,/Rail, A., Bed and Breakfasts, Small Inns and the Internet: The Impact of Technology on the Globalization of Small Businesses, *Journal of International Marketing*, 8, 2, 2000, pp. 86–97.
Lynch, P. D./Beck, J. C., Profiles of Internet Buyers in 20 Countries: Evidence for Region-Specific Strategies, *Journal of International Business Studies*, 32, 4, 2001, pp. 725–749.
Macdonald, S., Informal Information Flow and Strategy in the International Firm, *International Journal of Technology Management*, 11, 1/2, 1996, pp. 219–232.
Madsen, T. K./Servais, P., The Internationalization of Born Globals: An Evolutionary Process, *International Business Review*, 6, 6, 1997, pp. 561–583.
Networks and Informal Communication, *International Business Review*, 5, 2, 1996, pp. 137–150.
Marshall, P./McKay, J., Evaluating the Benefits of Electronic Commerce in Small and Medium Enterprises, *Australian Journal of Information Systems*, 9, 2, 2002, pp. 135–148.
McAuley, A., The Perceived Usefulness of Export Information Sources, *European Journal of Marketing*, 27, 10, 1993, pp. 52–64.
Mol, M. J./Koppius, O. R., Distance is not Dead: Why there is an L-Factor in Virtual Organisations, presented at the 25th Annual EIBA Conference, UMIST, Manchester, UK, December 1999.
Oxelheim, L., *Financial Markets in Transition. Globalization, Investment and Economic Growth*, London: International Thomson Business Press 1997.

Oxley, J./Yeung, B., E-commerce Readiness: Institutional Environment and International Competitiveness, *Journal of International Business Studies,* 32, 4, 2001, pp. 705–723.

Petersen, B./Welch, L. S./Liesch, P., The Internet and Foreign Market Expansion by Firms, *Management International Review*, 42, 2, 2002, pp. 207–221.

Piercy, N., Export Strategy: Key Markets vs Market Spreading, *Journal of International Marketing*, 1, 1, 1981, pp. 56–67.

Porter, M. E., Strategy and the Internet, *Harvard Business Review*, 79, 2, 2001, pp. 63–78.

Quelch, J. A./Klein, L.R, The Internet and International Marketing, *Sloan Management Review*, 37, Spring 1996, pp. 60–75.

Roche, E. M., Information Technology and the Multinational Enterprise, in Roche, E. M./Blaine, M. J. (eds.), *Information Technology in Multinational Enterprises*, Cheltenham, UK: Edward Elgar 2000, pp. 57–90.

Sarkar, M./Butler, B/Steinfield, C., Cybermediaries in Electronic Marketspace: Toward Theory Building, *Journal of Business Research*, 41, 3, 1998, pp. 215–221.

Seringhaus, F. H. R., The Role of Information Assistance in Small Firms' Export Involvement, *International Small Business Journal*, 5, 2, 1986, pp. 26–36.

Shapiro, C./Varian, H, *Information Rules.* Cambridge, MA: Harvard Business School Press 1999.

Tse, D. K./Gorn, D. J., An Experiment on the Salience of Country-of-Origin in the Era of Global Brands, *Journal of International Marketing*, 1, 1, 1993, pp. 57–76.

Vahlne, J-E./Johanson, J., New Technology, New Companies, New Business Environments and New Internationalisation Processes?, in Havila, V./Forsgren, M./Håkansson, H. (eds.), *Critical Perspectives on Internationalisation*, Oxford, UK: Elsevier Science 2002, pp. 209–227.

Vernon, R., International Investment and International Trade in the Product Cycle, *Quarterly Journal of Economics*, 80, 2, 1966, pp. 191–207.

Welch, D. E./Welch, L. S./Marschan-Piekkari, R., The Persistent Impact of Language on International Operations, *Prometheus*, 19, 3, 2001, 193–209.

Welch, L./Loustarinen, R., Internationalization: Evolution of a Concept, *Journal of General Management*, 14, 2, 1988, pp. 34–55.

Westbrook R./ Williamson, P., Mass Customization, *European Management Journal,* 11, 1, 1993, pp. 38–45.

Widdows, R./Widdows, K. L., Sisyphus at His Exercise: The Internet and Consumer Relations in the U. S., in Macdonald, S./Nightingale, J. (eds.), *Information and Organization*, Amsterdam: Elsevier Science 1999, pp. 215–228.

Wunderman, W., The Future of Selling via the Internet. The Online Progress of Disintermediation, *Web Commerce Today,* Issue 10, May 15, 1998. http://www.wilsonweb.com/wct1/980515wunderman.htm.

Yip, G. S., Global Strategy in the Internet Era, *Business Strategy Review*, 11, 4, 2000, pp. 1–14.

mir *Edition*

Laila Maija Hofmann

Führungskräfte in Europa
Empirische Analyse zukünftiger Anforderungen

2000, XXVIII, 414 Seiten, Br., € 64,00
ISBN 3-409-11704-0

Der europäische Integrationsprozess schreitet kontinuierlich voran. Die Autorin untersucht, inwieweit sich die Anforderungen an Führung in Unternehmen aus unterschiedlichen europäischen Ländern (noch) unterscheiden und welche Entwicklungen für die Zukunft zu erwarten sind. Aus den Ergebnissen in vier Regionen Europas werden Hinweise für die Gestaltung eines europäischen Personalmanagements abgeleitet, insbesondere für Führungskräfteauswahl und -entwicklung, sowie Konsequenzen für Nachwuchsführungskräfte.

Betriebswirtschaftlicher Verlag Dr. Th. Gabler GmbH, Abraham-Lincoln-Str. 46, 65189 Wiesbaden

Rajesh Chakrabarti/Barry Scholnick

Frictions in International E-Commerce[1]

Abstract

- Online book prices in USA and Canada convincingly reject the Law of One Price.
- Relative competitiveness is almost completely determined by the exchange rate.
- We conclude that extant frictions prevent the integration of the two national markets. We look into the possible causes of such friction and find that international shipping costs appear to be the most important hurdle.

Key Results

- Frictions in Cross-border e-commerce are large enough to prevent the Law of One Price and market integration.

Authors

Rajesh Chakrabarti, Assistant Professor of Finance, DuPree College of Management, Georgia Institute of Technology, Atlanta, Georgia, USA.
Barry Scholnick, Associate Professor of International Business, School of Business, University of Alberta, Edmonton, Alberta, Canada.

Rajesh Chakrabarti/Barry Scholnick

Introduction

In 1995, The Economist published a survey article – "The Death of Distance" (The Economist 1995[2]) – which predicted that because of the Internet, the transactions costs or frictions involved in doing international business would be significantly reduced in many industries. Six years later, the same magazine published a cover story – "The Internet's New Borders" (The Economist 2001) – arguing that "Geography matters in the networked world, and now more than ever". The differences in these articles reflect much of the changes in the discussion of international E-Commerce. Initial predictions of enhanced international commerce and increased globalization via the Information Superhighway have given way to skepticism about how "frictionless" the International e-commerce could become.

The issue of transactions costs has been a central part of the International Business literature. It is sometimes argued that the key difference between doing business in one country and many countries is the significantly increased transactions costs. In the standard IB context however, the discussion of transactions costs have usually revolved around the theory of the multinational, and in particular issues of international market entry, multinational firm size etc (for example Anderson and Gatignon 1986, and many others). International E-Commerce however presents a very different set of issues than the standard IB analysis. While the Internet may have reduced some barriers to International Business, other frictions may still remain. Determination of the existing frictions and their effect on international e-commerce, therefore, constitute an important research agenda.

In this paper we study the question of frictions in international e-commerce by examining the behavior of prices of identical products sold online by e-retailers in two different countries – in other words we test the Law of One Price (LOP) on the Internet. In a perfectly frictionless world where national markets are completely integrated and where a consumer is only "a click away" from purchasing foreign products, it may be argued that prices would tend to converge between sellers in different countries after adjusting for exchange rates. Difference in prices or significant variation in relative prices as a result of exchange rate movements, would indicate lack of market integration and the persistence of frictions in international business.

Using an innovative data collection methodology we build a unique dataset, drawing data directly from the web sites of the two companies. We build up a time series-cross section panel of the listed prices from each company for 3550 books, collected weekly for 57 weeks, resulting in a database of over 200,000 price observations for each store. A unique ISBN (International Standard Book Number) identifies each book. We thus have an opportunity to test the Law of One Price in the case of a *completely homogenous* product—a situation difficult to come across in most such comparisons. This allows us to compare the prices of exactly identical products offered on two different websites, in two different countries.

The main results of the paper are as follows. In broad terms, the prices charged at the two sites are relatively close to each other once corrected for the exchange rate. However, statistically, these prices convincingly reject the Law of One Price. In the dynamic context too, book prices fail to adjust to exchange rate movements. We interpret this failing of the Law of One Price as evidence of frictions in international e-commerce – frictions probably arising from various kinds of transactions costs. We discuss some of the possible sources of such friction that may still be evident in this market.

Motivation

There is a vast literature on the Law of One Price in the "old economy" context – examining whether traditional markets in different countries are integrated or not (see Rogoff 1996). The overwhelming conclusion in this literature is that Law of One Price is rejected which implies that markets in different countries are not integrated, and that there are considerable frictions in crossing international borders. Froot, Kim, and Rogoff 1995, for instance, strongly reject the Law of One Price for numerous commodities using European data for over 700 years. They argue that the rejection of the Law of One Price is one of the "most striking empirical regularities" (Froot/Kim/Rogoff 1995, p.1). In a less rigorous way, the Economist's regular MacPPP index also finds that the prices of MacDonald's hamburgers vary considerably in different countries after accounting for exchange rates. An important reason for this widespread failure of the Law of One Price is the presence of transactions costs[3].

The prerequisites of the Law of One Price include the absence of transaction costs. It assumes that agents can actually carry out a profitable cross-border goods arbitrage and profit from them in case of divergence in the prices of a product in two countries. The presence of real life transactions costs, therefore, create a band around the price of a product in a country within which international arbitrage is not profitable and hence Law of One Price cannot hold. Such transactions costs can be notionally broken down into two categories – 'search costs' and 'fulfillment costs'. The former refers to the fact that customers in a country rarely have the information about a lower priced similar product in a foreign country and acquiring that information may be inordinately expensive particularly if the product in question is a retail item. The latter includes cross-border shipping, tariffs and customs and other costs that may add to the price of an imported good.

Another feature that may prevent the Law of One Price is international price discrimination by producers—i.e. charging different prices in different countries according to local elasticities of demand to maximize total revenue. However, this too has its roots in transactions costs. Price discrimination is viable only if markets can be effectively segmented so that a buyer in the higher-price market cannot access the cheaper market[4].

While both categories of transactions costs are important in the conventional "bricks-and-mortar" world, 'search costs' are minimal in the world of e-commerce. A Canadian customer, for instance, can compare prices of books (or several other products) at Amazon and Chapters with just a few clicks of her mouse – physical distance and national borders are completely irrelevant here. This leads to the question: do prices in an online environment, free of 'search costs', satisfy the Law of One Price. This is the subject of the present paper.

In order to investigate these issues we provide a clinical study of the pricing behavior for two competitors, each a leader of e-commerce in its own country, selling a common commodity (books) in two neighboring countries, Canada and the US. The companies are Amazon.com, the world leader in e-commerce from the US, and Chapters Online, the leading Canadian online vendor. Amazon.com is among the world's largest Internet retailers and is almost synonymous with the idea of buying books online. Chapters Online is the leading online retailer in Canada across all product categories.

This case study is of particular interest because it focuses on an industry and a geographical area that would tend to have lower transactions costs than most others. The Canadian and US economies are highly integrated, with each being the other's most important trading partner. For the most part, there are very few cultural differences between Americans and English-speaking Canadians. Furthermore, books constitute a product category with no quality difference and have been one of the most successful product categories to sell online. The setting therefore, is purportedly biased towards the Law of One Price. If the LOP is violated in such a favorable setting, it is likely to fail in almost all other contexts of international e-commerce.

Chapters, Amazon and Online Book Retailing in Canada

Chapters Online, the online counterpart of the leading Canadian book-chain Chapters Inc., dominates the online book-retailing segment in Canada. Started in April 1999, it has a customer base of over half a million consumers (Chapters Online 2000) and offers over 2.5 million titles for sale (Shaw 2000). It is also by far the largest online Canadian vendor across all product categories (Chapters Online

2000). One of the major competitors of Chapters Online is the American firm, Amazon.com. Founded in 1994, Amazon is by far the world's largest online bookseller. It has over 3 million titles on offer, which is approximately 15 times larger than any conventional bookstore (Hof 1998) and its revenues from books alone is far in excess of that of its nearest competitor, Barnes & Noble.com (various SEC filings (10-K) available at www.edgar-online.com).

Given their relative ages and sizes, Chapters Online is clearly the newer entrant into the Internet bookselling market, competing with a dominant incumbent Amazon. Nevertheless Chapters is competitive with Amazon particularly among Canadian consumers. According to a recent Internet survey of Canadian online shoppers, 26% bought from Chapters while only 5% bought from Amazon (Pollara 2000).

While the effects of international competition in online retailing may exist on both sides of the border, given the smaller size of Chapters and its exclusively Canadian name recognition as well as the powerful brand-name of Amazon on the internet, it is more likely that Canadian shoppers would compare prices at the two outlets than American consumers. Amazon is an international player with operations in Europe and Japan in addition to the US while Chapters is largely Canadian. This is indeed reflected in the fact that Amazon is among the most visited e-commerce sites in Canada while Chapters has attracted few visitors from the US (Mediametrix 2000). Therefore this study focuses on price competition in the Canadian market.

It may be relevant to emphasize here that online retailing is an extremely competitive area with very thin margins (see Rosen/Howard 2000) where 'critical mass' is the crucial determinant of success or failure. It is also an area with marked 'winner takes all' features as described in Shapiro and Varian (1999).

Relationship to Previous Research

Online international competition among retailers is a recent phenomenon, as are most other e-commerce activities. This paper is among the first attempts to research this particular field. However, the area stands at the intersection of at least three broader areas, each of which has been widely researched in the past – international price and trade comparisons particularly in the US-Canada context; internationalization of retailing; and online retailing and e-commerce.

International price comparisons and the Law of One Price (or the related issue of purchasing power parity) have had a long and rich history in international economics research. Rogoff (1996) provides an excellent survey of this literature. In particular Isard (1977) finds that the "law of one price", one of the most important totems of international economics, is "flagrantly and systematically violated by empirical data". More often than not, transaction costs, that prevent international arbitrage, are at the root of these deviations from the textbook approach to international trade. In a recent paper, Obstfeld and Rogoff (2000) show that transaction costs may hold the key to several major puzzles of international economics. In this paper we examine both of these issues – the validity of the law of one price and the nature of cross border transaction costs – in the context of e-commerce.

US-Canada comparison of prices and trade volume has been a widely researched area in international economics. McCallum (1995), by comparing trade flows across the US-Canada border to those within Canada, finds that the border acts as a significant barrier to trade, in spite of the Free Trade agreement and the close cultural ties between the countries. Engel and Rogers (1996) find higher cross-border variation than within-country variation in price levels for identical categories of goods implying a significant border effect in the determination of prices. Helliwell (1998) corroborates these US-Canada 'border effect' findings using a much more extensive database of trade, prices, capital market linkages and labor flows. In particular, he concludes that "there are effectively no short-run price-equalizing pressures across national borders, even at the shortest distances" (pp.68). We examine this issue specifically in the E-Commerce environment.

The retailing sector has traditionally been one of the most non-traded of industries by the very nature of its activity. Selling to customers in foreign countries has been, as Salmon and Tordjeman (1989) point out, "partial and marginal". Before the advent of the Internet, all attempts at international expansion by a retailer necessarily involved either an alliance with a retailing chain abroad or heavy foreign direct investment. Nevertheless, Akehurst and Alexander (1995) find that there has been a rising trend in international retailing. Simpson and Thorpe (1995) and Williams (1992) provide surveys of the recent literature in the area. The most important reasons for the limited internationalization in the retailing sector are the large transaction costs, particularly search costs and shipping costs. This paper examines the nature of cross-border retailing in the online environment where search costs are expected to be significantly lower.

The advent of the internet and the increasing popularity of e-commerce has generated a rapidly growing body of literature focused on online retailing, particularly book retailing. Kotha (1998) and Kotha and Rindova (1999) study Amazon's business strategy and its reputation-building efforts. Bailey (1998), by comparing conventional and online prices for books, CDs and software, finds greater dispersion in prices of homogeneous goods on the internet than in traditional stores. Brynjolfsson and Smith (2000) study prices of books and CDs at conventional stores and the internet. Bakos and Brynjolfsson (1999) look at optimal bundling strategies for selling information goods on the Internet. Lynch and Ariely (2000) focus on the online wine market to study the effect of reduced information search cost in online shopping for a differentiated product. While most of the existing research in this new area has studied online retailing in a domestic setting, the present paper is among the first to take this line of inquiry to the international context.

Data and Data Collection

The data set we use in this paper comprises weekly observations on the prices of 3550 books from the two stores for a period of 57 weeks. Existing e-commerce research (see Bailey 1998 and Brynjolfsson/Smith 2000) has used much smaller databases to study online price competition. The data collected here come entirely from publicly available information on the Internet. The data collection technique is outlined below.

The product specifications for a book (i.e. the physical characteristics of a book) are completely captured by what is known as the International Standard Book Number or the ISBN of a book. The book market, therefore, provides us with a setting where the products being sold in the two countries in question are *exactly* identical – a feature that is difficult to obtain for most other product categories. In order to construct our dataset of books, we begin by building a sample of ISBNs obtained from an online book-selling site "even better.com"[5] – a source independent of the two bookstores under study. From the list of books available at this site, we generate a large sample of ISBNs of books belonging to different subject categories using proportionate random sampling. This involves picking up the same proportion of books from each of the different categories provided by the site[6]. Such proportionate sampling leads to the sample being more representative of a heterogeneous population like that of books.

Next we use a 'bot' – a web based program specifically designed for this purpose – which automatically extracts the necessary information for each book in our sample from the two websites, once every week (every Monday night). Our data, therefore, is weekly in frequency and covers the period from March 20, 2000 to April 22, 2001. We select the 3550 books for which data is available for all variables over the entire 57 week time period.

Prices at Amazon and Chapters cannot be compared without converting them to a common currency. We obtain the weekly Canadian Dollars – US Dollars exchange rate from OANDA (www.oanda.com) and use these figures to convert the Amazon prices to Canadian Dollars.

Both stores use incentives and follow "loyalty causing strategies" to lead to more return purchases. During the period under study Chapters used a "Chapters Club" program where members get a discount on their purchases. Amazon used promotional offers, gift certificates on selected products. While such programs may have some impact on effective prices, we do not consider them here as they are not universal in scope and it is not possible to estimate the effective price without knowing the details of individual sales. One thing is clear though. Such incentives are not biased to favor domestic customers over foreign customers and hence do not affect cross-border price comparisons.

Data Analysis and Results

The focus of our study in this paper is the extent to which Law of One Price (LOP) holds in the world of e-commerce. For this purpose, we compare both the price levels (in Canadian Dollars) at the two online retailers as well as study the evolution of these prices over the time period under consideration.

Price levels and the LOP

A standard way to test the presence of the Law of One Price is to regress the prices on one another and test if the coefficient is significantly different from unity (see Miljkovic 1999). We begin our analysis, therefore, by regressing the Chapters price on the Amazon price using the entire 200,000 plus observations for each variable in our sample. The choice of the dependent variable is motivated by the notion that Chapters is a significantly smaller competitor from a smaller country competing against the world leader in the industry. Our conclusions, of course, are invariant to the choice of the dependent (and independent) variable.

The estimated coefficient of Amazon price (in Canadian dollar terms) is 0.91. Because of the extremely large sample in this regression, the t statistic for this coefficient is very large (2034). The 95% confidence interval for this estimate is (0.913, 0.915). A likelihood ratio test rejects the hypothesis of the coefficient being equal to 1.0 at a 1% level. Thus there is clear statistical evidence of violation of Law of One Price in our data indicating the presence of frictions in international online retailing.

Figure 1 presents a scatter plot of the average price (average over 57 weeks) for the books in our sample at the two online retailers. It essentially provides a visual representation of the regression finding described above. Under the assumption of the Law of One Price, the book prices should have been along the 45° line (the dotted line in the figure). The figure shows that while the prices of the books in the two countries clusters around the 45° line, the regression line actually deviates significantly from the 45° line illustrating the violation of the Law of One Price.

Figure 1. Scatter Plot of Average (over 57 weeks) Prices at Chapters and Amazon for 3550 books

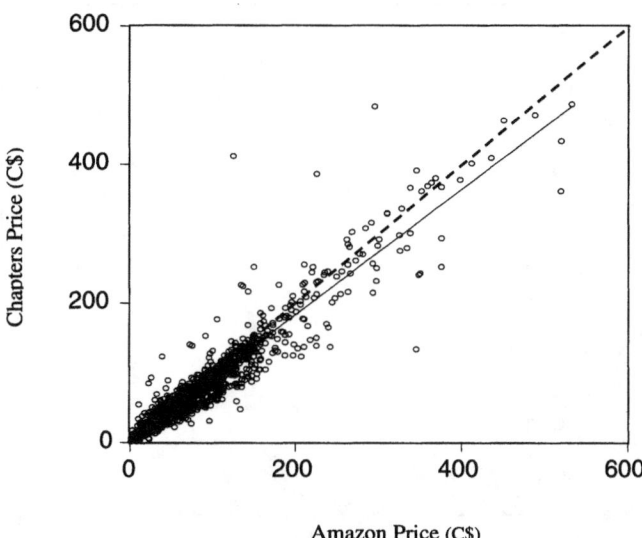

In order to get a better sense of the distribution of the relative book prices in the sample, we next present a histogram of the distribution in Figure 2. Here we obtain the relative book prices by dividing the average price (over 57 weeks) at Amazon (converted to Canadian dollars) by the average price at Chapters. A relative price of 1.0 indicates the Law of One Price in action. Removing a few (34) outliers to get a better visual sense of the distribution, we then create the histogram in Figure 2. The histogram reveals significant variation in relative book prices (the range of relative book prices in the entire sample is from 0.19 to 4.6). Thus, there are, in fact, books for which the average price in one online store is over four or five times that in the other. Also the distribution of relative prices is positively skewed suggesting that, while Chapters charges a small premium on most books, it also sells some books at large discounts as compared to Amazon.

Dynamics Over Time

While the absolute Law of One Price is statistically rejected by our sample, it is important to look at a relative version of the LOP as well. If the Law of One Price held in a relative sense, then this would mean that prices in the two stores would adjust to any changes in the exchange rate so as to keep the relative prices constant (even if not at unity). In other words, the "real exchange rate" for books between Canada and the USA should remain constant and variations in the US-

Figure 2. The Distribution of Relative Prices between Amazon and Chapters

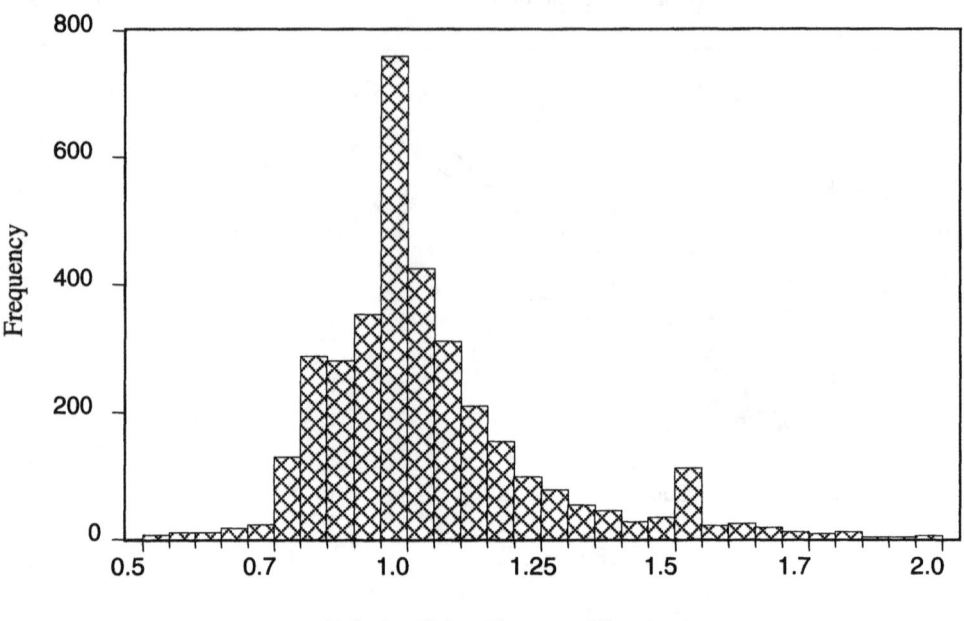

Relative Price (Amazon/Chapters)

Canada exchange rate should not have a prominent impact on it. The key question here is to what extent book prices react to changes either in the international competitor's price or in the exchange rate.

Figure 3 presents the data on the movement in the relative price of books at the two stores (Amazon price in Canadian dollars divided by the Chapters price). Because we are studying the temporal characteristics of the data here, we use average book prices (average for the 3550 books in our sample) for both stores for every week in order to compute the relative prices. The US-Canada exchange rate (US$ per C$) is also plotted in the same figure. During the period under study both variables experience variations close to 10% of their mean value. Thus the relative prices are far from constant. Nor are their movements independent of the exchange rate movements – a corollary of the Law of One Price. The extent of co-movement between the two variables is evident from the figure. The correlation between them is over 0.93 and when used in a regression, exchange rate movements account for about 87% of the temporal variation in relative book prices. This is clear evidence that Law of One Price does not hold even in a relative sense in the world of international online retailing. Book prices are clearly far more 'sticky' than the exchange rate even in the online environment where one would expect significantly reduced menu costs and hence prices to be more responsive to the exchange rate.

Figure 3. Movements in Relative Price and Exchange Rate (57 Weeks)

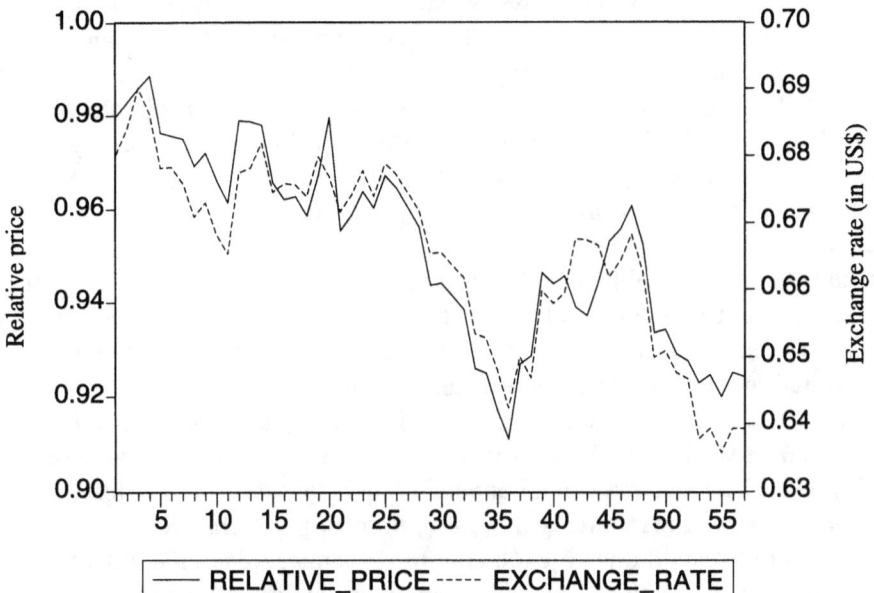

Price Changes in the Two Stores

In an integrated market, competing sellers are likely to react to one another's price changes. By this token if the online book retailing markets in the US and Canada are integrated, we should expect to see price movements by one seller in response to the other. Since Amazon is clearly the market leader, it is logical to expect that Chapters would exhibit some price-following behavior in response to changes made by Amazon. This is particularly true because price changes are much simpler to execute in online retailing. As opposed to the bricks and mortar stores all that an online vendor needs to change the price of a book is to change a number in a database. In other words, menu costs are thought to be significantly lower.

In this sub-section, therefore, we study the price changes made by the two online competitors in our sample. The aim is to examine, for each of the books, how often prices are adjusted and if there is a relationship between these adjustments. For these calculations we use raw nominal prices of each book in each country rather than an exchange rate adjusted price for one of the countries. This is because the multiplication of a price by the flexible exchange rate will distort any measure of price adjustment or volatility over time.

Table 1 shows the changes made in book prices at the two stores over the 57 weeks under consideration at the two stores. For approximately half of the 3550 books examined, if one of the stores has changed its price the other store had *not* changed its price. In 36% of the books, Amazon has changed its price and Chapters has not, and in 13% of the books, Chapters has changed its price and Amazon has not. There is thus no price-following pattern in the data. Also Chapters appears to be changing prices much less than Amazon does. This is in clear contradiction of the hypothesis that Chapters is a price follower since in that case Chapters would be reacting not only to Amazon's price changes but also to changes in exchange rate leading to more changes in Chapters prices than in Amazon prices.

It is, however, conceivable that Chapters is following a complicated price follower strategy under which it changes prices of some other books in response to Amazon's price changes. In order to study this possibility, we compute the coefficient of variation (standard deviation/mean) for each book in the two stores over the 57 weeks. The average of these 3550 coefficients of variation turns out to be 3.9% for Amazon while for Chapters it is less than 1.9%, i.e. less than half the figure of Amazon's. The correlation between them is less than 0.11. Clearly then Chapters does not even respond significantly, to most price changes at Amazon, not to speak about responding to exchange rate changes. The analysis of price changes in the two stores clearly reveals the lack of leader-follower relationship between the two stores, at least in prices.

To sum up, the key results from our analysis of the book prices are as follows. We find that the Law of One Price is clearly violated in book prices at the two major online retailers in two countries with the best chances for market integration. The real exchange rate in terms of books, or the common currency relative price is far from constant with its variations almost entirely explained by exchange rate movements – further proof of the violation of Law of One Price and hence lack of market integration. Finally, there is no evidence of price leadership between the two leading competitors, further confirming the finding of lack of market integration.

Table 1. Price Setting Behaviors in the Two Online Stores

	Amazon No Price Change	**Amazon** Some Price Change
Chapters No Price Change	972 Books (27.3%)	1303 Books (36.7%)
Chapters Some Price Changes	469 Books (13.2%)	803 Books (22.6%)

Possible Sources of Friction

The preceding section establishes that the Law of One Price is violated in the US-Canada online book retailing industry indicating that the two markets are not integrated, presumably because of transactions costs and frictions that have traditionally prevented the integration of national markets in the "old economy". The view that the online environment would render such transaction costs completely ineffective, if not totally eliminate them, is clearly not borne out by our data. In this section we describe some of the possible sources of such friction that still presents barriers to cross-border E-Commerce.

Shipping Costs

A key element of the new economy is the very "old economy" notion of getting the product shipped to the final consumer. An examination of both the Amazon and Chapters web sites indicates that shipping costs are a key area where national borders do indeed matter for E-commerce. In 2001, in order to ship one book from Amazon to a US customer the cheapest price is US$3.99, but to ship that same book to a Canadian customer the cheapest cost is US$5.48 (or approximately $8.22 in Canadian dollars). For a Canadian customer to purchase one book from Chapters the price is C$ 5.40. Thus for a Canadian consumer the price of shipping one book is C$2.82 cheaper if the book is shipped from the Canadian store rather than the US competitor.

The existence of this shipping cost premium of C$2.82 clearly gives Chapters an advantage in selling to Canadians. It should be pointed out, however, that the shipping cost differential of C$2.82 is relatively small relative to the average Chapters book price of approximately C$46.00 (i.e. approximately 6% of the average purchase price). In essence, Chapters does have a competitive "buffer" against Amazon because of the shipping cost differential, but this is a relatively small buffer. At the same time, the relatively small size of the shipping cost differential (on average 6% of the average Chapters price) may explain why Chapters feels it has to price many of its books broadly in line with the Amazon price, particularly if online shoppers fail to notice the shipping cost differential.

Morwitz et al. (1998) demonstrate that buyers routinely underestimate partitioned prices (i.e. an extra price such as a shipping cost). To what extent this is true online, particularly given that shipping costs are often revealed at a much later stage in the buying process, remains an interesting empirical question. However, our data suggests that Chapters is hesitant to take advantage of the full "buffer" it enjoys, perhaps because of this reason.

Consumer Search Costs

Another transaction cost that has been thought to influence pricing behavior on the Internet is the notion that for a consumer shopping on the internet, the comparison of prices between different competitors is only "a click away", even though the competitors may be in different countries. It is this idea that search costs have become very small for consumers, that has driven the prediction of "frictionless" e-commerce where a firm could not afford to charge a price that was higher than its competitor.

Recent research on consumer behavior on the Internet has examined the issue of whether or not consumers actually do search for multiple prices before making a purchase. Johnson et al. (2001) have provided data that consumers in their sample only visit on average approximately 1.1 internet bookstores. They explain this by arguing that consumers, after a while, learn about a particular store or layout of that store on line and then return again and again to that store. If this hypothesis is correct for a proportion of consumers then there may be less pressure for storeowners to rapidly adjust prices for every book when the price changes at the competitor store. In our context, for instance, experienced Canadian online shoppers may not compare prices at Amazon, if they have found that prices on average in the past have been more or less comparable.

However, given that a store does not know how many people may follow this non-searching behavior, and how many may indeed search for the best price, it would seem consistent with the observed pricing behavior that prices are broadly in line on average. There is also the possibility that a few sophisticated online shoppers may even be using "shop-bots" that automatically hunt for best bargains, though international shop-bots are still hard to come by. Thus divergence from Law of One Price, though clearly present, is unlikely to exceed a reasonable level.

Menu Costs

A related transaction cost that was thought to disappear with the advent of e-commerce are menu costs. These are simply the costs involved in changing the prices displayed to the consumer. In a perfectly frictionless world where each store would rapidly adjust prices in response to any change in the competitor's price, or even the exchange rate, menu costs would be assumed to be very low. Indeed, menu costs are likely to be much lower for online vendors than their traditional counterparts and it is even possible to have the prices programmed in such a manner that they automatically adjust to the competitor's moves and other factors. Nevertheless, with a store selling products such as books, with millions of different prices to adjust, widespread price revisions may indeed be far from costless.

It is interesting to note that of the 3550 books in our sample, Amazon changed the price at least once of 64% of the books over the course of 57 weeks, while Chapters changed the price at least once of only 40% of the same books over the 57 weeks. These data have a number of interesting implications.

If it is argued that Chapters is a much smaller store that is based only in the Canadian market, and is attempting to halt the increased sales of its much larger American based competitor, then one would expect that Chapters would have to be particularly responsive to changes in price by Amazon. Furthermore, it can be argued that Chapters will also have to respond to any shifts in the US Canadian exchange rate. For all of these reasons, therefore, one would expect that Chapters would adjust its prices much more readily than Amazon.

One possible reason for why Chapters in fact does not adjust its prices as much as Amazon is that for a smaller store such as Chapters it does not have the resources to rapidly adjust all the prices that its competitors adjust. If this where indeed the case then it could indicate that menu costs may not in fact be irrelevant for E-Commerce. Of course, as discussed above, it is also possible that Chapters does not adjust its prices as often as Amazon because it has a shipping cost differential in its favor – as discussed above. Given the nature of our data, it is not possible to make a definitive statement on this issue. However this issue is clearly an important topic of further research.

Protectionist Barriers – No Longer a Barrier on the Internet

Finally, the US-Canada book retailing sector does indicate the disappearance of an important and much discussed friction to International Business – that of protectionist government policies. This particular case study of the international E-Commerce market for books in Canada and the US provides an interesting example of how protectionist barriers can be circumvented by e-commerce outfits.

Under the Canada-US free trade agreement as well as the North American Free Trade Agreement (NAFTA), the government of Canada was able to negotiate an "exemption" to free trade, and Foreign Direct Investment into Canada for what it defined as "Cultural Industries". Essentially, these measures provided protection to Canadian companies from competition from US based companies. Cultural Industries are very broadly defined and they include bricks and mortar bookstores. Thus in the mid 1990s, when the US based bookstore Borders was set to enter the Canadian market by building a large chain of bookstores, the Canadian government, on extensive lobbying by Canadian bookstores such as Chapters, stopped this using the "cultural exemption clause" of the NAFTA. This effectively protected the Canadian book market from the entry of US booksellers.

The advent of international E-Commerce, however, has rapidly changed the marketplace for books in Canada. The NAFTA provision that stops US firms from investing in Canada, obviously has no validity for the book market on the Internet, where US companies do not make any investment in Canada, but merely ship books across the border from bases in the US.

Thus, the advent of the Internet has been important for reducing the effect of protectionist barriers such as those imposed by the Canadian government in the book retailing industry. The reduction of this potentially very large friction is consistent with our finding that prices charged on the Internet by Amazon and Chapters are broadly similar. The remaining sources of friction, however, are sufficient to prevent complete market integration and hence the Law of One Price is still violated.

Conclusions

In this paper we study the nature of international price competition in the online book retailing industry – one of the most important segments of B2C e-commerce. We examine if the Law of One Price operates between the leading online book retailers in the USA and Canada, a situation most favorable for the operation of the Law of One Price. We compare weekly prices for a sample a 3550 books over a period of 57 weeks at Amazon and Chapters Online, the leading online book retailers in the USA and Canada respectively and analyze these prices to test the Law of One Price.

We find that our data clearly contradicts the Law of One Price in levels with statistically significant difference in prices between the two stores. In the dynamic setting we find that the common currency relative price for books does not stay constant over the period under study – as would have been expected if the Law of One Price held in a 'relative' sense. The variation in this 'real exchange rate' in books is almost completely explained by movements in the US-Canada exchange rate during this period, indicating that book prices are far more 'sticky' than the exchange rate. Finally, there is no evidence that Chapters actually changes its prices in reaction to price changes initiated by the industry leader Amazon. In fact Chapters turns out to be changing prices far less frequently than Amazon.

We interpret all this evidence as indicative of lack of integration between two neighboring national markets separated by what is perhaps the most porous border anywhere outside the Euro area and faced with the least degree of cultural difference. If the Law of One Price fails under circumstances most favorable to it, it is only likely to be even strongly violated in other international business contexts.

The claim that the Internet has made the world of International Business 'frictionless' is, therefore, exaggerated at best. Frictions continue to keep national markets separated even in the online environment.

We next describe a few possible sources of friction that may be preventing complete market integration. International shipping costs appear to be an important hurdle that drives a wedge between prices in two countries. In our study, Amazon's shipping costs to Canada as compared to Chapters, where able to some extent to erode its competitiveness in the Canadian market. We also argue that search costs and menu costs, may still be present in the online environment.

While these forms of friction continue to prevent integration of national markets, the advent of the Internet has at least circumvented a much more important hurdle, protectionist government policies. Indeed the Canadian book market is out of bound for US bricks and mortar chains because of the protectionist policies of the Canadian government – policies that are completely toothless against international online sales. The Internet has thus opened up certain hitherto protected markets. However, completely 'frictionless' international business has not yet emerged – even on the Internet.

Endnotes

1 We would like to thank Chris Studholme and Rahul Ravi for excellent research assistance and two anonymous referees for helpful comments.
2 An extended version of the Economist article is also published under the same title and under the name of the Economist journalist as Cairncross (1997).
3 In the case of many commodities like hamburgers, the presence of differently priced "non-tradable" inputs – like real estate prices – that, by definition, cannot be arbitraged away, also contributes to the failure of the Law of One Price in a significant manner.
4 Sometimes it is also achieved through cosmetic changes in the product but that is not applicable to books, the commodity under study here, because we are comparing identical books with identical ISBN numbers.
5 The original address of this site was www.evenbetter.com. However, during our study it was acquired by a more general comparison shopping site, DealTime.com (www.dealtime.com).
6 These categories are: Antiques & Collectibles, Architecture, Art, Biography & Autobiography, Body, Mind & Spirit, Business & Economics, Computers, Cooking, Crafts & Hobbies, Current Events, Drama, Education, Family & Relationships, Fiction, Foreign Languages Study, Games, Gardening, Health & Fitness, History, House & Home, Humor, Juvenile Fiction, Juvenile Nonfiction, Language Arts, Literary Criticism & Collections, Mathematics, Medical, Music, Nature, Performing Arts, Pets, Philosophy, Photography, Poetry, Political Science, Psychology & Psychiatry, Reference, Religion, Science, Self Help, Social Science, Sports & Recreation, Study Aids, Technology, Transportation, Travel and True Crime.

References

Anderson, E./Gatignon, H., Models of Foreign Entry: A Transaction Cost Analysis and Propositions, *Journal of International Business Studies*, Fall 1986, pp. 1–26.
Akehurst, G./Alexander, N., Developing a Framework for the Study of the Internationalization of Retailing, *Service Industries Journal*, 15, 4, 1995, pp. 204–209.
Bailey, J. P., *Intermediation and Eelectronic Markets: Aggregation and Pricing in Internet Commerce*, Ph.D. Thesis (Technology, Management and Policy), MIT 1998.
Bakos, Y./Brynjolfsson, E., Bundling Information Goods: Pricing, Profits and Efficiency, *Management Science*, 45, 12, 1999, pp.1613–1630.
Brynjolfsson, E./Smith, M., Frictionless Commerce? A Comparison of Internet and Conventional Retailers, *Management Science*, 46, 4, 2000, pp.563–585.
Cairncross, F., *The Death of Distance: How the Communications Revolution Will Change Our Lives*, Boston, MA: Harvard Business School Press 1997.
Chapters Online 2000, Annual Report (www.chapters.ca/ir)
The Death of Distance, *The Economist*, September 30, 1995.
The Internet's New Borders, *The Economist*, August 11, 2001.
Engel, C./Rogers, J., How Wide Is The Border? *American Economic Review*, 86, 5, 1996, pp. 1112–1125.
Froot, K./Kenneth, M. K./Kenneth, R., The Law of One Price Over 700 Years, NBER Working Paper, No. 5132, 1995.
Helliwell, J. F., *How Much Do National Borders Matter?*, Washington, D.C.: Brookings Institute Press 1998.
Hof, R., Amazon.com: The Wild World of E-Commerce, *Business Week*, December14, 1998, p. 37.
Isard, P., How Far Can We Push the Law of One Price?, *American Economic Review*, 67, 5, 1977, pp.942–948.
Johnson, E./Moe, W./Fader, P./Bellman, S/Lohse, J., On the Depth and Dynamics of Online Search Behavior, Columbia University Working Paper 2001.
Kotha, S., Competing on the Internet: How Amazon.com is Rewriting the Rules of Competition, *Advances in Strategic Management*, 15, 1998, pp. 239–265.
Kotha, S./Rindova V., Building Reputation on the Internet: Lessons from Amazon.com and its Competitors, University of Washington Business School, Working Paper, 1999.
Lynch, J. G./Ariely, D., Wine Online: Search Costs and Competition on Price, Quality and Distribution, *Marketing Science*, 19, 1, 2000, pp. 83–103.
McCallum, J. National Borders Matter: Canada-US Regional Trade Patterns, *American Economic Review*, 85, 3, 1995, pp. 615–623.
Morwitz, V. G./Greenleaf, E./Johnson, E. J., Divide and Prosper: Consumers' Reactions to Partitioned Prices, *Journal of Marketing Research*, 35, 4, 1998, pp. 453–463
Mediametrix, Media Metrix Canada Press Releases, www.mediametrix.ca 2000.
Miljkovic, D., The Law of One Price in International Trade: A Critical Review, *Review of Agricultural Economics*, 21, 1, Spring-Summer 1999, pp. 126–139.
Obstfeld, M./Rogoff, K., The Six Major Puzzles in International Macroeconomics: Is There a Common Cause? *National Bureau of Economic Research*, Working paper 7777, 2000.
Pollara, Pollara Internet Survey, Canadian Internet Holiday Spending Exceeds Expectations, (www.pollara.ca) 2000.
Rogoff, K., The Purchasing Power Parity Puzzle, *Journal of Economic Literature*, 34, 2, 1996, pp. 647–668.
Rosen, K. T./Howard, A. L., E-Retail: Gold Rush or Fool's Gold?, *California Management Review*, 42, 3, 2000, pp. 72–100.
Salmon, W. J./Tordjman, A., The Internationalisation of Retailing. *International Journal of Retailing*, 4, 2 , 1989, pp. 3–16.
SEC Filings (10-K), various years, available at www.edgar-online.com

Simpson, E. M./Thorpe, D. I., A Conceptual Model of Strategic Considerations For International Retail Expansion, *Service Industries Journal,* 15, 4, 1995, pp. 16–24.

Shapiro, C./Varian H.,. *Information Rules: A Strategic Guide to the Network Economy,* Boston, MA: Harvard Business School Press 1999.

Shaw, H., Curbing Costs Key to Chapters Online, *National Post*, September 8. (www.nationalpost.com) 2000.

Williams, D. E., Retailer Internationalization: An Empirical Inquiry, *European Journal of Marketing,* 26, 8, 1992, pp. 8–24.

mir Edition

Andreas Wald

Network Structures and Network Effects in Organizations

A Network Analysis in Multinational Corporations

2003, XVIII, 238 pages, pb., € 49,90 (approx. US $ 49,90)
ISBN 3-409-12395-4

Network structures have been praised as the organizational form of today's multinational corporation. Building on conceptual work on network organizations, a quantitative network analysis of formal and informal organizational structures is performed in this study. It is tested whether network structures can be identified empirically. Moreover, the effects of organizational structures on strategic decision making in two multinational corporations are analyzed. A theoretical framework is provided by an exchange model and by social capital theory.

The book is addressed to scholars of international management and organizational studies.

Betriebswirtschaftlicher Verlag Dr. Th. Gabler GmbH, Abraham-Lincoln-Str. 46, 65189 Wiesbaden

mir Special Issue 2003/1, pp. 51–71

Management
International Review
© Gabler Verlag 2003

Thomas C. Lawton/Steven M. McGuire

Governing the Electronic Market Space: Appraising the Apparent Global Consensus on E-Commerce Self-regulation

Abstract

- This paper explores the developing regulatory regime for e-commerce to understand why private sector modes of regulation have attained prominence in policy debates. We draw from theoretical work on regulatory development and utilize a framework constructed by Braithwaite and Drahos (2000) to test a hypothesis about firm activism.

- We examine firm – government interactions in both the US and the EU to determine whether firms succeeded in getting their regulatory preferences adopted.

Key Results

- We find that evidence for firm 'first-mover' success is equivocal. Firms often succeed in getting their preferences adopted because governments are already predisposed towards a pro-market approach.
- International governmental consensus on e-commerce self-regulation is not nearly as cohesive as rhetoric suggests. We find two levels of complexity: first, there is an EU-US difference in the expectations of self-regulation; and second, self-regulation is more readily accepted for some aspects of e-commerce than for others.

Authors

Thomas C. Lawton, Senior Lecturer in International Business Strategy, School of Management, Imperial College Management School, London, UK.
Steven M. McGuire, Lecturer in International Business, School of Management, University of Bath, UK.

Thomas C. Lawton/Steven M. McGuire

Introduction

The economic significance of the electronic economy for international business, together with its social and technological ramifications and transborder nature, have generated significant debate about the role of government in the new market space. Cogburn argues that, when dealing with issues that are transnational in scope, the quandary is how to achieve significant levels of global governance in the absence of a global government (2001, p. 23). This is not a new problem – it has arisen in the past for areas such maritime commerce (Cafruny 1987) and telecommunications (Cowhey Aronson 1993, Zacher/Sutton 1996). Nonetheless, it is a relevant and immediate dilemma, in need of an appropriate and timely solution.

In the early days of the e-economy, the idea that cyberspace could be governed was treated with derision. It was argued that, in this fast-paced and borderless world, states would be unable to tax and too slow to regulate and so the new economy would come close to being a pure market. Moreover, state authority was, in culture and operation, antithetical to the 'spirit' of cyberspace. Barlow (2001) spoke for many when he commented:

> 'Governments of the Industrial World, you weary giants of flesh and steel, I come from Cyberspace, the new home of the Mind. On behalf of the future, I ask you of the past to leave us alone. You are not welcome among us. You have no sovereignty as we gather.'[2]

The regulatory framework for e-commerce is chaotic: there are numerous international organizations, national governments and trade associations producing reports, studies and policies. There is little agreement about the operational details of e-commerce regulation.[3] Yet, there is one area of broad consensus: private regulation will be preferred to public, on balance. In 1997, several countries, including Australia, the US and Canada – but also developing states such as Colombia and Egypt – agreed to a set of general principles regarding e-commerce. The first principle was that the private sector should lead; other principles specifically encourage industry self-regulation and call on governments to avoid 'unnecessary restrictions on electronic commerce' (Mann et al. 2000, p. 170). The WTO's seminar on e-commerce regulation in 1999 came to the same conclusion. The Chairperson remarked that one of the conclusions of the seminar was that maximum reliance had to be placed on self-regulation of e-commerce. Government intervention, though inevitable, must have a 'light touch' (WTO 1999, p. 21).

This paper addresses one fundamental question: how did this broad consensus on the primacy of self-regulation come into being? We are interested in understanding how, amid all the confusion surrounding e-commerce and the seemingly diverse interests of developed and developing states on these issues, the preference for a market-led approach is so widespread. In doing so, the paper aims to throw light on business – government interactions in the development of regulation for the growing electronic economy.

Research Methodology

This paper draws on primary documentation from the US, the EU and the WTO, as well as publications of important private sector groups such as the Global Business Dialogue on E-commerce (GBDe) and the Business and Industry Advisory Committee (BIAC) to the Organisation for Economic Co-operation and Development (OECD). In addition, interviews were conducted with a sample of expert witnesses. This sample comprised a group of high-level representatives from business, government, international organisations, and NGOs (primarily trade union and consumer lobby groups). Interviewee selection was, for the most part,[4] premised on participation in the seminal 1998 OECD ministerial conference on e-commerce and was designed to obtain a wide variety of perspectives (van der Heijden 1996). The 1998 conference, held in Ottawa, was one of the first significant international gatherings of governments, firms and civil society actors to discuss e-commerce regulatory co-ordination. Many of those interviewed argued that the meeting made a significant contribution to the discourse and policy that subsequently emerged on e-commerce. Initial research identified 48 conference delegates as potential interviewees. Further research reduced this number to 32 feasible interview candidates. All were subsequently contacted and of these, 16 failed to respond, 4 refused interviews and 12 agreed. Based on the original target sample, this is a 25 per cent response rate. Adjusted to eliminate the one-third who proved non-contactable, the response rate increases to 37.5 per cent.

Developing the Framework: Firms, States and Regulation

Braithwaite and Drahos (2000) note that government regulations are often nothing more than state adoption of what had been prevailing practice among firms. In this view, state policymaking tends merely to formalize what were already widely practiced and broadly accepted norms of private economic actors (p. 492). But can this argument help us understand e-commerce regulation? One problem is the novelty of electronic commerce itself; it is by no means clear that the industry has developed the set of norms and practices that governments will then adopt as formal regulation. This informal process is buttressed by an appeal to expertise or the technical demands of the industry, which tend to favour industry-led solutions.

In examining the developing regulatory regime for electronic commerce, it is helpful to consider the extent to which firms are, or were, activists in favour of particular policies. An extensive body of literature already exists in support of the notion that firms can and do influence the public policy agenda on a regular and ongoing basis (Richardson/Jordan 1979, Streeck/Schmitter 1984, Junne 1992, Mazey/Richardson 1993, Verwey 1994, Green-Cowles 1995, Lawton 1996, 1997, Baron 1999, Kyrou 2000). Braithwaite and Drahos clearly acknowledge the important role of activist firms in developing certain policies. Similar to Sabatier's (1987) and Sabatier and Jenkin-Smith's (1993) advocacy coalition concept and to Culter, Haufler, and Porter's (1999) notion of private regimes, Braithwaite and Drahos (2000) develop a framework that clarifies how private regulatory entrepreneurship can shape policy outcomes. In stage one, a key individual, firm or organization identifies a problem requiring a regulatory solution. Stage two involves the enlistment of organizational power; it is at this stage that new interest groups are formed, or existing ones energized, and strategies and tactics developed for 'selling' the preferred regulatory solution to authorities. Third, the preferred option is rejected, accepted or modified in the policy-making process of key states. Finally, the preferred outcome is globalized. This model is a useful tool for conceptualising the proactive involvement of private sector actors in the evolution of an international regulatory framework for e-commerce. A simplified version of the Braithwaite and Drahos framework is shown below.

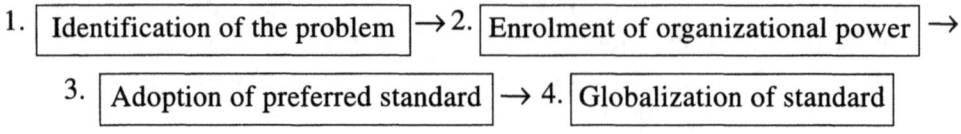

Adapted from Figure 23.2, in Braithwaite and Drahos (2000), p. 562.

A substantial body of work exists to provide an understanding of how business lobbies pressed for an extension of WTO rules to services (Ryan 1998, Sell 2000, 2001, Stegemann 2000). The inclusion of intellectual property right (IPR) provisions in the Marrakesh Treaty owes an enormous amount to the determined efforts by American multinationals to gain international protection for their patents and copyrights. More generally, firms succeeded in convincing governments that 'services' were tradeable across borders, and that investment issues required multilateral rules to constrain states on matters like expropriation (Sell 2000, p. 174).

The WTO was the preferred arena for these efforts as other agencies, such as the World Intellectual Property Organization (WIPO) lacked robust dispute settlement procedures (Stegemann 2000, p. 1238). However, the key insight of Sell is to understand that firms do not always succeed in getting their preferences accepted. In her analysis of financial services, GATS, TRIPS and TRIMS, Sell notes that these agreements vary in the extent to which they offer protection for business: 'The US private sector actively pushed for all these agreements, so the variation in outcomes suggests that private authority is not triumphant in all areas.' (2000, p. 174). What conditioned this success? First, firms seemed to have the most success when they were able to mobilize transnationally (Risse-Kappen 1995, Michaels 2001). In particular, when American and European firms developed a common position, it was more difficult to block proposals. Second, while transnational membership is important, it also seems crucial that the private sector proposals are coherent, feasible and consistently pressed. It took two decades for IPRs to be accepted by the US government as a legitimate topic for multilateral negotiations. Finally, governments must be persuaded. In multilateral forums like the WTO, developing states have some bargaining power (Panagariya 2000). In the case of intellectual property rights, trade-offs with other issues, such as textiles, helped secure agreement.

A different perspective arises from the work of Spar (2001). Spar argues that in the early phases of regulatory innovation, firms often take the lead. This is because they alone understand the operations and limitations of the technologies underpinning the new sector. These are the pioneer firms brave enough to enter a new sector in an effort to gain a first mover advantage. However, as Spar notes, governments get involved at some point; indeed they often do so at the request of firms. This is because sophisticated markets require rules. Once e-commerce becomes a viable *technology*, it needs a social and legal framework to make it a viable *industry*. Indeed, firms come to see how government regulation can actually protect the gains these firms have made by creating rules that reflect the preference of this select group of firms.

Drawing on this work, we develop the following working hypothesis: *Self-regulation is the dominant mode because firms succeeded in gaining a first mover advantage in determining e-commerce regulation*. For this hypothesis to be true, it would have to be evident that firms really dominated the input side of the process in the US and other countries from the mid-1990s. In comparative terms, this hypothesis comes closest to the case of intellectual property rights in Sell's work. In that case, a group of American TNCs formed a specialist lobby group, the Intellectual Property Committee (IPC) with the expressed purpose of getting IP protection into the WTO process. The IPC mobilized European and Japanese firms in support of a coherent set of principles. The transnational private lobby in turn succeeded in persuading OECD governments of the position. The WTO TRIPs agreement represents that successful globalization of this preferred standard.

Thomas C. Lawton/Steven M. McGuire

Why Self-Regulate? The Theoretical Backdrop

As an increasing number of firms globalise their operations, they encounter a myriad of regulatory regimes in everything from competition policy, health and safety standards to planning regulations. Complying with these regimes pose two problems for firms. First, and most obviously, they represent a cost. Second, they can affect the competitiveness of firms by shaping the market into which a firm enters. Domestic firms can retain a competitive advantage over new entrants if the regulatory regime – deliberately or not – makes it difficult for firms to contest the market. This is why the private-sector bias in e-commerce regulation is so interesting; if it is everything it appears, it represents an interesting attempt to make global e-commerce relatively contestable through the adoption of common standards. The self-regulatory agenda represents a nascent attempt at global standardization of e-business in preference to national or regional adaptation.

What does self-regulation mean in practice and what advantages and disadvantages are there to employing a predominantly self-regulatory framework for the global electronic market space? Olson (1965) provides the genesis for self-regulation as a management concept and business phenomenon, when he first refers to the notion of self-organised attempts at collective action, without direct intervention by the state. Huyse and Parmentier (1990) refer to the self-regulation process as 'subcontracting', whereby the state limits its role to establishing the formal conditions for rule making and leaves it up to the non-state actors to determine the regulatory content and emphasis.

Private or self-regulation can be viewed as a supplement, substitute or delegate of the state (Boulding 2000, p. 135, King/Lenox 2000, p. 698, Price/Verhulst 2000, p. 59). Regulation is formalised along a scale of three primary organisational means of controlling business behaviour: government organisation, industry self-organisation and market organisation (Price/Verhulst 2000, p. 59). Government or public regulation ('command and control') is the most formal, where non-compliance may lead to legal sanctions.[5] Market organisation ('laissez faire') is the least formal, where compliance is voluntary (Sinclair 1997, p. 529). In practice, these three forms overlap and often combine due to the complexity of modern business and society. Formal command and control regulation is frequently combined with self-regulation in cases of market or policy failure or jurisdictional ambiguity. Hoffman-Riem (1996) terms this 'regulated self-regulation'. Price and Verhulst (2000) refer to it as 'two-tiered regulation', which they contend is particularly relevant in business sectors that are complex and transnational in nature. E-commerce clearly fits into this category, indicating that a two-tiered or regulated self-regulatory approach may be one option for the electronic economy.

Price and Verhulst (2000, p. 65) further subdivide self-regulation into four distinct forms, which differ in scope and arguably determine the ultimate success or failure of a self-regulatory process.[6] The first form is mandated self-regulation, where a business sector is forced by government to formulate and enforce norms within a framework that is defined and policed by the state. The second is sanctioned self-regulation, in which the sector itself formulates the rules but these are subject to government approval. A third type is coerced self-regulation, wherein business develops a set of norms and standards in response to an implied or explicit threat by government to introduce statutory regulation. The fourth variety is voluntary self-regulation, where the state has no active involvement. In the case of e-commerce, self-regulation is coerced, as business is hastening to determine its own rules and procedures before government introduces a clear and comprehensive regulatory regime. The transnational nature of e-commerce necessitates some degree of international consensus on regulation. This is a task which – as we will see further on – is proving elusive. Failure to reach regulatory harmony between states allows business greater scope for determining an effective and internationally agreed self-regulatory regime for e-commerce.

The Development of E-Commerce Regulation

Corporate interests were represented in e-commerce policy-making from the early days of the Internet's utilisation for commercial purposes. Most notably, in the US, the Computer Systems Policy Project (CSPP) was influential in the early debates surrounding the nature of e-commerce regulation.[7] The CSPP was formed in 1989 as a public policy advocacy group on issues such as international trade and, subsequently, Internet taxation and e-commerce. Its membership comprised the Chairmen and Chief Executives of the US's leading information technology companies.

Under the leadership of Ira Magaziner, the US government embarked on a consultation exercise in 1995 to formulate policy toward e-commerce, with firms, as well as NGOs being part of the process. By 1997, the process had generated a loose consensus on the nature of e-commerce regulation: given the global nature of the technology, self-regulation would be an important cornerstone for any regulatory regime.[8] Thus, a key recommendation was that the US government would:

> encourage the creation of private fora to take the lead in areas requiring self-regulation such as privacy, content ratings, and consumer protection and in areas such as standards development, commercial code and fostering interoperability (White House 1997, quoted in Green-Cowles 2001a)

Similar consultative processes were occurring elsewhere. In the UK, the threat of criminal action against Internet service providers (ISPs) in respect of web-based pornography produced a government – business agreement to create an independent NGO to monitor and inform regulation. The goal for UK-based ISPs was to pre-empt more extensive government regulation by creating a code of practice for firms.[9] The EU too, embarked on a consultation exercise.

Clear efforts to create a transnational private lobby to affect electronic commerce first became evident in 1997. This effort built on earlier activities by national and regional private sector bodies that had developed positions on the issue. It is also clear that business lobbies broaden their contacts with state authorities by engaging actively in the WTO's e-commerce studies. Prominent associations in this process were: the Business International Advisory Committee of the OECD (BIAC); the International Chamber of Commerce (ICC); the TransAtlantic Business Dialogue (TABD) and, subsequently, TABD's affiliate, the Global Business Dialogue on E-commerce (GBDe).

BIAC is a unique organization in that it has an institutionalised relationship with one of the principle intergovernmental organizations for economic governance, the OECD. BIAC was formed in 1962 and as the OECD's Director-General notes, 'BIAC is closely involved and making valuable contributions in areas as diverse as tax reform, bribery and corruption, corporate and public governance regulatory reform, competition policy, electronic commerce and financial markets' (BIAC 1999, p. 2). BIAC works to 'help governments resist the temptation to act before understanding fully a new problem' (BIAC 1999, p. 7).

Another key actor was the TransAtlantic Business Dialogue (TABD).[10] Established in 1995 at a US-EU conference in Seville, the TABD was a relative newcomer to international lobbying, but it rapidly established a successful track record. Green-Cowles argues that 'the TABD is intrinsically part of the transatlantic regulatory negotiating process. . .[it] blurs the traditional distinction between public and private governance' (2001b, p. 214). Business leaders were pleased with the influence afforded them through the TABD. BASF Chairman Jurgen Strube commented:

> 'We have been pleased with the four-way business-to-government partnership that has evolved through this process'.[11]

The brainchild of then US Commerce Secretary, Ron Brown, and EU Commissioners, Leon Brittan and Martin Bangemann, the TABD's main interest lay in the further synchronization and liberalisation of EU-US commercial relations. More specifically, the harmonisation of standards and certification, increased trade and investment liberalisation and the co-ordination of regulatory policy were at the forefront of the TABD's agenda. The 'regime'[12] therefore unsurprisingly became interested in the evolving e-commerce debate. Like BIAC, TABD supported e-commerce self-regulation, arguing that international co-operation for the development of policies that support the growth of e-commerce must be industry-led and encourage industry self-regulation (TABD 1998, p. 1). TABD set up a special e-commerce committee in 1997, which was under the co-chairmanship of Les Alberthal of EDS and Bertelsmann's Thomas Middlehoff (Green-Cowles 2001a, p. 8). The early meetings featured an extraordinary consensus among industry' in respect of self-regulation for e-commerce: a consensus that contrasted to the differences between the EU and US governments (Green-Cowles 2001a, p. 9).

The final key corporate actor was the International Chamber of Commerce (ICC). The ICC is one of the oldest business associations in the world and the breadth of its activities is unusual: it not only lobbies but also runs the International Court of Arbitration (Kelly 2001, Schneider 2000). The ICC was concerned about the proliferation of potential global regulators of e-commerce, arguing that at least 18 international organisations are working on e-commerce issues. In an effort to shape this process and develop a larger role for self-regulation, the ICC has developed a global action plan to sell a business perspective on which international or supranational organisations should do what. This agenda is based on the US National Information Infrastructure of 1993, the Global Information Infrastructure Initiative of 1995, and the 1997 White House report, *A Framework for Global Electronic Commerce* (Braithwaite/Drahos 2000, p. 112).

By mid-1997 an intensive consultative process on e-commerce regulation was underway on both sides of the Atlantic – offering an opportunity for firms and NGOs to react to the EU's draft directive on e-commerce and the US's Framework document. A major meeting in Bonn in July 1997 revealed a high degree of consensus among European and American firms about the desired trajectory of regulation (Green-Cowles 2001a, p. 7).[13] However, differences soon emerged between European and American government officials about the scope of self-regulation. While TABD and GBDe officials were able to maintain broad corporate agreement, the European Commission, whilst accepting a place for self-regulation, articulated a clear willingness for state regulation where needed (Green-Cowles 2001a, p. 7, EU 1997).

In 1998, an OECD ministerial conference was held in Ottawa on the theme of 'A Borderless World: Realising the Potential of Global Electronic Commerce'. The conference brought together not only OECD ministers but also observers from non-OECD countries, business leaders, labour representatives, and consumer and social interest groups. This meeting is widely perceived as having made an important contribution to the development of e-commerce regulation discourse and policy.[14] Some delegates described it as the 'specifically most effective' conference on e-commerce regulation to date.[15] Business lobbies took this opportunity to form the Alliance for Global Business: a consortium of five international business organizations including BIAC, the ICC, the Global Information Infrastructure Commission (GIIC), the International Telecommunications Users Group

(INTUG) and the World Information Technology and Services Alliance (WITSA). Although non-business NGOs were invited and participated in the discussions, several delegates doubted that NGO input carried as much weight as business. 'You just had to look at the amount of corporate sponsorship associated with the event' one delegate noted.[16]

In the months before the conference, business associations and individual firms embarked on an intense consultation process. As participants pointed out, at high level conferences like the OECD ministerial the important issues are negotiated and – to the greatest extent possible – agreed before anyone even arrives for the conference.[17] The Global Business Dialogue on E-commerce (GBDe), TABD's affiliate on electronic economy issues was influential insofar as it brought prominent CEOs into the process. However, the GBDe's capacity to translate its prominence into policy was doubted in some quarters. The fine detailed work of developing draft rules and policy papers soon fell more to the ICC: a task made easier by the high degree of consensus among firms about the self-regulatory agenda.[18]

The Alliance's policy document, *Global Action Plan for Electronic Commerce* (1998, 1999) is one of the most conclusive and cooperative statements in support of e-commerce self-regulation and flowed from the perception that business needed to present a more 'robust' message to policymakers (BIAC 1999, p. 7). Early drafts of the document were circulated at the conference and acted as the basis for discussion in many sessions.[19] The preference for self-regulation was evident in the introduction:

> 'Throughout history, business has set its own standard rules and practices to lower transaction costs, to avoid and resolve conflicts and to create consumer confidence'.[20]

In the first edition (1998), the Global Action Plan urged governments to rely on business self-regulation. In the second edition, the plan argues that the pace of change and nascent state of e-commerce have heightened the risks associated with premature or unnecessary government regulation (1999, p. 6). The action plan calls for a 'hands-off' approach by government on certain issues. The report acknowledges that government intervention may be required on matters of intellectual property protection, taxation and the removal of barriers to competition in providing the underlying infrastructure. However, a clear preference is expressed for self-regulation in most other matters (1999, p. 7).

On the face of it, the Ottawa OECD Ministerial Conference was a success for the Alliance for Global Business.[21] The conference concluded that first, public policy for e-commerce should be a co-operative and inclusive process (involving all interested governmental, private sector, and civil society players); second, policy and regulatory actions should strive to be internationally compatible whenever possible; and third, governments should promote a pro-competitive environment and work to eliminate barriers to trade (OECD 1998, pp. 4–5). Significant emphasis was placed on ensuring legal clarity and consistency for global e-commerce. Agreement was also reached on the role of government vis-à-vis firms in the development and control of e-commerce: the private sector should take the lead role in e-commerce development and should continue to extend self-regulatory mechanisms. On taxation, it was agreed that business would continue to work with the OECD to ensure that neutrality is the guiding principle and that taxes are not imposed in a discriminatory manner.

In spite of the Ottawa conference's conclusion that e-commerce policy should be a co-operative and inclusive process, civil society did not appear to be equal partners in the process. Consumer lobby representatives at the conference[22] argue that the Ottawa agenda was clearly dominated by business interests and that it was not until the creation in late 1999 of the Transatlantic Consumer Dialogue (TACD)[23] that consumer influence began to increase. However, some NGO/civil society representatives[24] argue that the agenda did shift from a strong pre-conference bias in favour of self-regulation to a more balanced post-conference approach.

The results of the Ottawa Ministerial seem to feature a clear preference for self-regulation on customer service matters, with firms acknowledging a role for government in providing the legal and tax infrastructure. In other words, while lobby group documentation proclaims a preference for market-led solutions, this phrase must actually be unpacked. Relationships with customers – which rely primarily on soft issues of trust and credibility – can be safely governed with self-regulatory codes. Another area where self-regulation has been embraced is Alternative Dispute Resolution (ADR). Governments accepted that the special environment of e-commerce presents a challenge to traditional means of dispute settlement:

> The global nature of e-commerce, however, complicates this issue because the choice of law, jurisdiction and liability rules vary significantly among countries... Even if issues of applicable law and jurisdiction could be adequately resolved, international private litigation over small-value internet transactions does not make practical or economic sense... For this reason, the Administration has promoted collaborative efforts among the private sector and consumer groups to develop and implement fair and effective Alternative Dispute Resolution... (USGPO 1999, p. 36)

Interestingly, the GBDe accepts that, in theory, 'complete international harmonization of applicable laws' would be the best solution, but impractical given the difficulties of reconciling national laws and cultures (GBDe 2001, p.6). ADR is advanced not out of simple aversion to government regulation – though the costs of traditional courts are a consideration – but as a practical, self-regulatory response to an international collective action problem.

Research Findings: Did Business Lead?

This paper seeks to explain the apparent consensus in favour of self-regulation for electronic commerce. The work of Braithwaite and Drahos (2000), Sell (2000), Spar (2001) and others is used to develop a conceptual framework for understanding how business had its regulatory preference accepted by state power. In this framework, business groups identified a policy area and formulated a preferred policy option. The second stage of this process, however, is the most important. As Michaels (2001) and Sell (2000, 2001) argue, business groups enjoy the greatest success when they are able to create a transnational coalition in favour of their regulatory preference. 'The transnational leadership of the Intellectual Property Committee was *decisive* in the achievement of the TRIPS accord' (Sell 2001 p. 197, emphasis added). However, as Sell notes, leadership in this context requires the maintenance of a clear set of policy goals, well articulated to government over time.

Does the framework help us to understand the growth of self-regulation in e-commerce? The answer is equivocal. There was clearly a transnational business lobby in favour of self-regulation, which arises in the late 1990s.[25] This lobby was successful at gaining access to policymakers and appears influential. However, unlike the intellectual property case that underpins our framework, there is no clear evidence that governments were accepting a particular regulatory solution that they would not otherwise have done.[26] The IPC convinced a sceptical US government about the advantages of global IPR; by contrast, the US government appeared quite willing from the outset to accept self-regulation for at least some aspects of electronic commerce. The first US government draft of an e-commerce strategy proposal appeared in December 1996. President Clinton's *A Framework for Global Electronic Commerce* and the *Presidential Directive on Electronic Commerce* followed this in 1997. Both documents stated very clearly that the private sector should lead any and all e-commerce regulatory initiatives and that government involvement should be minimalist and largely supportive in nature. Ira Magaziner, senior policy advisor to the Clinton Administration and architect of the US government's original e-commerce policy, argues unequivocally that at least in the US, government precipitated the discourse and regulatory agenda on e-commerce. Moreover, from the outset, the federal government advocated a fundamentally self-regulatory approach. The government's underlying rationale stemmed from its early identification of e-commerce – lightly regulated and allowed to grow – as a key component in the furtherance of US competitiveness, both in domestic and global markets.[27]

The lack of evidence in support of the firm activism hypothesis therefore suggests a different explanation. In this alternative hypothesis we would argue that governments actually started the process in favour of self-regulation – or were at least comfortable with adopting private regulation as a regulatory 'default mode'. This can be explained from a Gramscian international political economy perspective that claims modern state power is closely aligned with capitalism (Gill 1998). In short, it might be the case that state authorities accepted the primacy of e-commerce self-regulation not because of corporate lobbying, but because they neither considered nor favoured alternative approaches. The evidence suggests that, although disagreement existed on the self-regulatory remit, the US, EU, Japan, Australia and others all agreed that self-regulation was a positive approach to governing the commercialisation of the Internet.[28]

Spar offers a more process-oriented explanation. When creating regulations for new sectors, governments often turn to firms, particularly the early entrants – 'pioneers' as Spar calls them – as the only source of information upon which to make policy (2001, xxv). Net Shepherd, an early entrant into the electronic economy, was invited by the Canadian government to inform e-commerce policymaking because the firm was an early developer of filter and search technologies on the Internet. Other interviewees agreed: the early phases of e-commerce regulation are characterised by collective uncertainty. In this environment, pioneer firms have a key role to play.

However, while self-regulation is broadly accepted, the *degree* of acceptance varies. At the rhetorical level, many actors, both private and public, express a desire for the private sector regulation of e-commerce. However, at the level of detail, a more complex picture emerges. First, there is disagreement among key state actors about the precise scope of private sector dominance. The key player here is the EU, represented by its quasi-executive body, the European Commission. The EU favours the coordination and liberalization of e-commerce governance but its policies are the least acceptant of self-regulation.[29] In 1997, when the EU began consultations on e-commerce regulation, NGOs as well as firms had access to the process. One NGO representative was quite content with the level of access his organization achieved.[30]

This reluctance is rather durable and is reflected in the EU's legislation; the 2000 Directive on Electronic Commerce appears little changed from the 1997 draft. The 2000 Directive placed considerable emphasis on the role of government as Internet regulator and e-commerce promoter. This divergence from the US position reflects what Turner (2000) describes as an 'EU-US culture clash' on matters relating to internet regulation. At the core of this disagreement is the EU's tendency to place less confidence than the US places in the ability of the market to regulate itself (Turner 2000, p. 142).[31] For instance, the e-commerce law most quickly adopted in the US was on copyright and intellectual property rights.[32] All laws imposing obligations on business – data protection, sales tax and so forth – have seen much slower progress in the US. In the EU, by contrast, more legislation has been adopted in parallel. For instance, data protection has existed for some time and V. A. T. (sales tax) on e-commerce came into force in early 2002.

This may be attributable to a clear divide between the US and the EU on their respective approaches to consumer protection.[33] The US argues against any legislation that cannot be clearly enforced. Enforcement continues to be a problem in the disintermediated and global world of e-commerce. The EU generally favours[34] more immediate legislative guidelines on issues such as consumer privacy, in the belief that cumulative and transborder legislation will contribute to the emergence of a coherent and cohesive international system for policing of the Internet.

The clash, or more accurately, difference of emphasis, may also be summarised as a US preference for some form of governance and a European preference for actual government (Rosenau/Czempiel 1992). Other work on EU commercial policies suggests that the European Commission remains more autonomous from business influence than, for example, the US government (Coen 1999, Hocking/McGuire 2002). While this autonomy was overcome in the intellectual property case, there is no evidence that European firms lobbied hard for e-commerce self-regulation, perhaps because the Commission does accept the general argument for firm-led solutions.[35] How doe we explain this outcome? US – EU differences are important and do reflect historical and cultural traditions, but this should not be overstated: interviewees make it clear that EU proposals were *sufficiently* sympathetic to use of self-regulation to obviate the need for aggressive lobbying (Mann et al. 2000, p. 132).[36]

The EU-US differences on Internet regulation are not confined solely to political elites but have a cultural basis. Singh and Singh found that contrary to their European counterparts; the majority (76 per cent) of US consumers believe that 'the Internet industry' should police itself (2001, p. 12). Moreover, a similar trend can be found among businesses, with US firms' preferring little or no regulation while the opposite is true in Europe (Singh/Singh 2001, p. 13). Less than a quarter of US consumers support government intervention, despite the fact that they are beginning to view online privacy as a growing concern (Scheibal/Gladstone 2000, Singh/Singh 2001). Markoff (1998) argues that this weight of public opinion in the US in favour of e-commerce self-regulation influenced the Clinton Administration's reluctance to police the Internet and underpinned the government's support for self-regulation.

Finally, the paper has illustrated the need to unpack the term self-regulation: neither firms nor states accept Barlow's (cited in Kobrin 2001) vision of an unregulated Internet. There is indeed a broad consensus on the need for firm-driven regulation, but a more detailed analysis suggests that this desire varies according to the type of activity under discussion. It is clear that firms prefer self-regulation on operational matters such as interoperability, customer relations and dispute settlement. Arguments in favour focus first of all on firm self-interest: companies have a commercial interest in developing codes of conduct to counter customer reluctance to use the Internet. Second, with technology moving so rapidly it is assumed that government should not, or even could not, hope to develop appropriate regulations. However, as one pulls back from the customer, business becomes more comfortable to situate itself in state-based regulatory frameworks.[37] For example, the GBDe's recommendations for taxation do not call for a tax-free Internet: there is no suggestion that cyberspace cannot be taxed. Rather, the issues involve making e-commerce taxation fair, feasible and simple: in short, the same demands that many 'old economy' firms make about tax policy (GBDe 2001, p.71–73).

On this reading, the research tends to confirm Spar's argument about rule making: firms eventually appreciate and advocate some degree of government regulation so that economic gains from new activity can be protected. Any industry, 'needs property rights, and standards, and some basic understanding of what constitutes fair and foul play. And the only entity that can sustain and enforce these rules is the state.' (Spar 2001, p.294). Angelo Gennari, in his speech to the 1998 Ottawa conference likewise suggested that, for all the rhetoric surrounding self-regulation, once e-commerce began to take-off firms and governments would see the benefits of creating a stable and robust legal environment (Gennari 1998, p.12).

Conclusion

Assumptions about a globalised, private regulatory regime for e-commerce are clearly a long way off, despite considerable rhetorical support for a market-led approach. This paper endeavours to add to the literature on the role of firms in the development of regulatory regimes. It begins with the observation that there appears to be an international consensus for self-regulation. We have asked why this is the case. We then utilise other work (Brathwaite/Drahos 2000, Sell 2000, 2001, Spar 2001) in an attempt to structure our investigation of e-commerce regulation. As with the IPR case, we found evidence that there is a transnational coalition for e-commerce regulation. Structurally, similarities exist between the two cases but the process differs. We did not find tangible evidence that firm activism exists and that corporate actors dominate the process and have first mover advantage.[38]

However, two other findings emerge in this paper. First, those political actors that subscribe to the global consensus for self-regulation are not uniformly supportive of self-regulation at all times and for all issues. In particular, the EU does not possess the same confidence as the US in the ability (or willingness) of business to regulate itself. The EU advocates a more active role for government, particularly in support of consumer rights. A second, related finding is that self-regulation is not viewed – particularly by government – as a panacea for the monitoring of all e-commerce norms, procedures and practices. The term needs to be unpacked so as to distinguish between those issue areas where the sharing of responsibility within a business sector is the most appropriate course of action and those where government may play a useful role as independent arbitrator and protector of consumer or corporate rights. The control of e-commerce site content might be an example of the former and the protection of IPRs could fall into the latter category. This suggests that firms will have to continue to cope with a number of regulatory regimes for e-commerce. However, as EU-US clashes over privacy illustrate, different conceptions of the appropriate balance between market-led and state-led regulation can affect businesses. Firms need to remain alert and not assume that cyberspace is truly borderless.

Endnotes

1 Earlier versions of this paper were presented at the International Studies Association annual conference, New Orleans, Louisiana, 15 March 2002, the Irish Academy of Management annual meeting, Derry, Ireland, 6–7 September 2001 and at the Comparative Interdisciplinary Studies Section meeting of the International Studies Association, Heidelberg, Germany, 28–29 June 2001. The authors wish to thank all the participants at these meetings – particularly John Kirton, Daniel Papp and Benedicte Bull – as well as Eleanor O'Higgins, Gunter Walzenbach and the journal's referees and guest editor for their helpful comments on earlier versions of this paper.
2 Quoted in Stephen Kobrin (2001), *'Territoriality and the Governance of Cyberspace'*, *Journal of International Business Studies*, 32, 4, pp. 687–704.
3 Where no specific e-commerce rules exist, courts around the world tend to apply existing rules or use analogies in order to deal with disputes concerning e-commerce.
4 A number of interviews were conducted with experts who did not attend the 1998 Ottawa conference.
5 It should be noted that within civil law, there is still a clear distinction between private and public law. In civil law countries such as Germany, France and the Nordic states, private law comprises intellectual property rights, contract law and so forth, whereas public law consists of tax and competition legislation and issues relating to jurisdiction. It is possible to deviate from private but not from public law. In contrast, common law makes no distinction between private and public law. In common law countries such as the US and the UK, self regulation is usually limited to private law.
6 It should be pointed out that Price and Verhulst's subdivision of self-regulation does not fit very well in the context of law except for their last category: voluntary self-regulation which can be perceived as a situation where government has no need to intervene.
7 The importance of the CSPP was brought to our attention in a discussion with Dr Michael Nelson, former Special Advisor on Technology to US Vice President Al Gore (1993–1997).
8 Interview with Dr Ira Magaziner, former Senior Policy Advisor to President Clinton and director of the Clinton Administration's policy on the commercialisation of the Internet, 13 May 2002.
9 Interview with David Kerr, Chief Executive, Internet Watch Foundation, 7 May 2002.

10 TABD membership comprises more than 100 corporate executives from prominent US and EU companies, as well as high ranking officials from the EU and US administrations. Companies represented include Philips, Boeing, Federal Express, Pirelli, Nokia, Ford, IBM, Pfizer, Bayer and Unilever.
11 Mr Strube was quoted in a document titled 'The Transatlantic Business Dialogue' on the internet homepage of the United States Delegation to the European Union, www.useu.be/docs/tabd.html
12 We hesitate to describe the TABD as an organisation as it has neither an official structure nor a formal legal existence.
13 This was further established in an interview with Ira Magaziner, 13 May 2002.
14 The majority of those interviewed for this paper agreed with this assertion.
15 This comment was made by Dr Angelo Gennari, Head of Studies and Research, CISL (Italian Confederation of Workers' Trade Union) and member of the OECD Consultative Committee of Trade Unions, in an interview for this paper, 23 April 2002.
16 Interview conducted with Mr James Love, Consumer Project on Technology, Washington D. C., 25 April 2002.
17 Interviews with Ms Maria Livanos Cattaui, Secretary General, and Ayesha Hasson, Senior Policy Advisor, International Chamber of Commerce, 24 April 2002 and with Mr David Kerr, Chief Executive, Internet Watch Foundation, 7 May 2002.
18 Interview with Ms Cattaui and Ms. Hassan of the ICC, op cit.
19 This point was substantiated in an interview with Dr Angelo Gennari, op cit.
20 Cited by Gennari 1998, p. 5 in his speech at the Ottawa conference.
21 The importance of the Ottawa conference within the e-commerce regulatory process is substantiated by the 2000 *UK House of Lords Report on E-Commerce in Europe* which stated that the conference was a 'particular milestone in the international reaction to the new technology' (2000, p.1).
22 A vocal advocate of this position is James Love of the Consumer Project on Technology. Mr Love further contends that civil society remains quite weak relative to business, particularly in the US.
23 The TACD is a forum of US and EU consumer organisations that develop and agree joint consumer policy recommendations to the US government and the EU to promote the consumer interest in policy-making. Three committees were established within the TACD to deal with e-commerce issues. EU representatives argue that 'the TACD has been the primary forum of influence for civil society' (interview with EU official, 29 April 2002).
24 Trade union representative, Dr Angelo Gennari, op cit, made this point.
25 This argument was substantiated in interviews with a wide range of participants in the regulatory process. These included Dr Michael Nelson, Director of Internet Technology and Strategy at IBM and former Special Advisor on Technology to US Vice President Al Gore (24 April 2002); Dr Angelo Gennari, Head of Research and Studies at the Italian Confederation of Workers Trade Union (23 April 2002); Mr James Love, Consumer Project on Technology (25 April 2002); and a European Commission official (29 April 2002).
26 This point was substantiated in interviews with senior officials from both the Clinton Administration and the European Commission.
27 Ira Magaziner interview, op cit.
28 This agreement was evident from the policy documents produced by respective governments at this time and was confirmed in interviews with a number of both former and current EU and US officials, April-May 2002.
29 Discussions with EU officials reveal not hostility to self regulation *per se* but a long-standing EU commitment to more of a balance (than in the US) between self regulation and public regulation.
30 Interview with Mr David Kerr, op cit.
31 Interview with EU official, op cit.
32 Although it should be noted that this was followed closely by the Children's Privacy Protection Act.
33 Interview with Ira Magaziner, op cit.

34 There is not unilateral agreement on this approach within the EU, with countries such as France being more prone to a regulatory agenda and others, including the United Kingdom and Ireland, favouring less governmental control.
35 For example, the Commission has broadly accepted an ICC designed protocol for digital signatures. Interview with Cattaui and Hassan, op.cit.
36 Interviews with Cattaui, Hassan and Magaziner.
37 As former Clinton Administration advisor, Dr Michael Nelson, argued in an interview for this paper, a business-government consensus on the approach to regulation clearly emerged in the US during the 1990s. In areas such as tax and Internet crime, government should clearly take the lead. In areas including privacy and pornography, business should take the lead. This point was sustained in an interview with Mr Steve Gray of the Universal Postal Union, who argued that self-regulation has to be treated case by case and that there are some market areas where business should take the lead but others where government clearly has precedence.
38 This could of course be explained by the costs accrued by firms in the creation of a self-regulatory framework. It may therefore be argued from a transaction cost perspective that firms have a clear interest in governmental provision of a legal framework – provided they are satisfied with the content of the rules.

References

Baron, D., Integrated Market and Nonmarket Strategies in Client and Interest Group Politics, *Business and Politics*, 1,1, 1999, pp.7–34.
Boulding, M. E., Self-regulation: Who Needs It?, *Health Affairs*, 19, 6, 2000, pp. 132–9.
Braithwaite, J./Drahos, P., *Global Business Regulation*, Cambridge: Cambridge University Press 2000.
Business and Industry Advisory Committee to the Organisation for Economic Co-operation and Development, Global Information Infrastructure Commission, and International Chamber of Commerce, *A Global Action Plan for Electronic Commerce: Prepared by Business with Recommendations for Governments,* first edition, Paris: OECD 1998.
Business and Industry Advisory Committee to the Organization for Economic Co-operation and Development, *BIAC in Action: An Annual Report for 1999*, www.biac.org 1999.
Business and Industry Advisory Committee to the Organisation for Economic Co-operation and Development, Global Information Infrastructure Commission, and International Chamber of Commerce, *A Global Action Plan for Electronic Commerce: Prepared by Business with Recommendations for Governments,* second edition, Paris: OECD 1999.
Cafruny, A. W., *Ruling the Waves: the Political Economy of International Shipping*, Berkeley: University of California Press 1987.
Coen, D., 'The Importance of US Lobbying Practice on the European Business – Government Relationship', *California Management Review*, 41, 4, 1999, pp.27–45.
Cogburn, D. L., Global Governance in Cyberspace (or Did E-Commerce Kill the Net?), *International Studies Association* annual meeting, Chicago, IL, 20–24 February 2001.
Commission of the European Communities, *A European Initiative in Electronic Commerce*, Communication to the European Parliament, the Council, the Economic and Social Committee and the Committee of the Regions, COM(97) 157, 15/04/97, http://www.ispo.cec.be/Ecomerce 1997.
Council of the European Union, *Directive on Electronic Commerce*, Directive 2000/31/EC of the European Parliament and of the Council of 8 June 2000, Official Journal of the European Communities, L 178, 17.7.2000.
Cowhey, P./Aronson, J., *Managing the World Economy: The Consequences of Corporate Alliances*, New York: Council on Foreign Relations 1993.
Cutler, A. C./Haufler, V./Porter, T., (eds.) *Private Authority and International Affairs*, Albany: State University of New York Press 1999.

Federal Trade Commission, 'Federal Trade Commission Responses to Questions Regarding Electronic Commerce', House Committee on Commerce, US Congress, 9 November 1999, www.ftc.gov/os/1998/9804/blileyt.htm 1999.

Gennari, A., *Lead Intervenor for TUAC,* OECD Ministerial Conference on Electronic Commerce, Ottawa, 9 October, 1998.

Gill, S., 'New Constitutionalism, Democratisation and Global Political Economy', *Pacifica Review,* 10,1, February 1998, pp. 23–38.

Global Business Dialogue on E-Commerce, *GBDe Conference 2001: Tokyo Recommendations,* 14 September 2001.

Green-Cowles, M. Setting the Agenda for a New Europe: the ERT and EC 1992, *Journal of Common Market Studies.* 33,4, 1995, pp. 501–26.

Green-Cowles, M., 'Who Writes the Rules of E-Commerce: A Case Study of the Global Business Dialogue on E-Commerce', Policy Paper 14, American Institute for Contemporary German Studies 2001a.

Green-Cowles, M., 'The Transatlantic Business Dialogue: Transforming the New Transatlantic Dialogue', in Pollack, M./Schaffer, G. (eds.), *Transatlantic Governance in a Global Economy,* Lanham, MD: Rowman & Littlefield 2001b.

Hocking, B./McGuire, S., 'Government – Business Strategies in EU-US Economic Relations: The Lessons of the Foreign Sales Corporation Issue', *Journal of Common Market Studies,* 40,3, September 2002, pp. 449–470.

Hoffmann-Riem, W., *Regulating Media,* New York: Guilford 1996.

Huyse, L./Parmentier, S., Decoding Codes: the Dialogue between Consumers and Suppliers through Codes of Conduct in the European Community, *Journal of Consumer Policy,* 13, 1990, pp. 260–287.

Junne, G., Multinational Enterprises as Actors, in Carlnaes, W./Smith, S. (eds.), *The European Community and Changing Foreign Policy Perspectives in Europe,* London: Sage 1992.

Kelly, D., 'The Business of Diplomacy: The International Chamber of Commerce Meets the United Nations', Working Paper 74/01, Centre for the Study of Globalisation and Regionalisation, University of Warwick 2001.

King, A. A./Lenox, M. J., Industry Self-Regulation without Sanctions: the Chemical Industry's Responsible Care Program, *Academy of Management Journal,* 43, 4, 2000, pp. 698–716.

Kobrin, S., 'Territoriality and the Governance of Cyberspace', *Journal of International Business Studies,* 32, 4, 2001, p. 687–704.

Kyrou, D., *Lobbying the European Commission: The Case of Air Transport,* Aldershot: Ashgate 2000.

Lawton, T. C., Industrial Policy Partners: Explaining the European level Firm-Commission Interplay for Electronics, *Policy and Politics,* 24, 4, 1996, pp. 425–436.

Lawton, T. C., *Technology and the New Diplomacy: the Creation and Control of EC Industrial Policy for Semiconductors,* Aldershot: Avebury 1997.

Mann, C./Eckert, S./Cleeland Knight, S., *Global Electronic Commerce,* Washington D. C.: Institute for International Economics 2000.

Markoff, J., 'US and Europe Clash over Internet Consumer Privacy', *New York Times,* www.nytimes.com/library/tech/98/07biztech/articles, 1 July 1998.

Mazey, S./Richardson, J., *Lobbying in the European Community,* Oxford: Oxford University Press 1993.

Michaels, K. P., Opening Skies: The Political Economy of the Air Cargo Industry in the Philippines and Taiwan, unpublished Ph.D. Dissertation, The London School of Economics and Political Science, London, England 2001.

Ministry of International Trade and Industry, *Towards the Age of the Digital Economy: For Rapid Progress in the Japanese Economy and World Economic Growth in the 21st Century,* draft, Tokyo: Ministry of International Trade and Industry 1997.

Ministry of International Trade and Industry, *Towards eQuality: Global E-Commerce Presents Digital Opportunity to Close the Divide between Developed and Developing Countries (MITI's proposal for WTO E-Commerce Initiative),* second draft, Tokyo: Ministry of International Trade and Industry 2000.

Olson, M. *The Logic of Collective Action: Public Goods and the Theory of Groups*, Boston, MA.: Harvard University Press 1965.

Organisation for Economic Co-operation and Development [OECD] Ministerial Conference, *A Borderless World: Realising the Potential of Global Electronic Commerce*, Directorate for Science, Technology and Industry, SG/EC(98)14/Final, Paris: OECD 1998.

Organisation for Economic Co-operation and Development, *E-Commerce: Impacts and Policy Challenges*, Economics Department Working Papers No. 252 (Jonathan Coppel), Paris: OECD 2000.

Panagariya, A., E-Commerce, WTO and Developing Countries, *The World Economy*, 23, 8, 2000, pp. 959–978.

Price, M. E./Verhulst, S. G., In Search of the Self: Charting the Course of Self-Regulation on the Internet in a Global Environment, in Marsden, C. T. (ed.), *Regulating the Global Information Society*, London: Routledge 2000.

Richardson, J. J./Jordan, A. G., *Governing Under Pressure: the Policy Process in a Post-Parliamentary Democracy*, Oxford: Martin Robertson 1979.

Risse-Kappen, T., *Bringing Transnational Relations Back In: Non-State Actors, Domestic Structures and International Institutions*, Cambridge: Cambridge University Press 1995.

Rosenau, J. N./Czempiel, E.-O., (eds.), *Governance Without Government: Order and Change in World Politics*, Cambridge: Cambridge University Press 1992.

Ryan, M., *Knowledge Diplomacy: Global Competition and the Politics of Intellectual Property*, Washington: Brookings Institution Press 1998.

Sabatier, P. A., Knowledge, Policy-Oriented Learning and Policy Change: An Advocacy Coalition Framework, *Knowledge, Creation, Diffusion, Utilization*, 8, 4, 1987, pp. 649–692.

Sabatier, P. A./Jenkins-Smith, H. C., (eds.), *Policy Change and Learning: an Advocacy Coalition Approach*, Boulder, Co: Westview Press 1993.

Scheibel, W. J./Gladstone, J. A., 'Privacy on the Net: Europe Changes the Rules', *Business Horizons*, May-June 2000, pp.13–8.

Schneider, V., Global Economic Governance by Private Actors: the International Chamber of Commerce, in Greenwood, J./Jacek, H. (eds.), *Organized Business and the New Global Order*, Basingstoke: Macmillan 2000.

Sell, S., Big Business and the New Trade Agreements: the Future of the WTO?, in Stubbs, R./Underhill, G. (eds.), *Political Economy and the Changing Global Order*, Oxford: Oxford University Press 2000.

Sell, S., Private Power, Public Law: the Globalization of Intellectual Property Rights, unpublished manuscript, 2001.

Sinclair, D., Self-Regulation Versus Command and Control? Beyond False Dichotomies, *Law and Policy*, 19, 4, 1997, pp. 529–559.

Singh, J. V./Singh, J. 'E-Commerce in the US and Europe – is Europe Ready to Compete?', *Business Horizons*, March-April 2001, pp.6–16.

Spar, D., *Pirates, Prophets and Pioneers*, London: Random House 2001.

Streeck, W./Schmitter, P., (eds.), *Private Interest Government: Beyond Market and State*, London: Sage 1984.

Stegemann, K., The Integration of Intellectual Property Rights into the WTO, *The World Economy*, 23, 9, 2000, pp. 1237–1268.

TransAtlantic Business Dialogue, EU and US TABD Priorities in Electronic Commerce, TABD Statement, 23 April 1998.

Turner, C., *The Information Economy: Business Strategies for Competing in the Digital Age*, London: Kogan Page 2000.

UK House of Lords, *Select Committee on European Union – Fourteenth Report*, 25 July 2000.

United States Government (USGPO), *3rd Annual Report: US Government Working Group on Electronic Commerce*, Washington D. C.: USGPO 1999.

Van der Heijden, K., *Scenarios: The Art of Strategic Conversation*, Chichester: Wiley 1996.

Verwey, W., HDTV and Philips: Stepping Stone or Snake Pit?, in Pedler, R. H./Van Schendelen, M., (eds.), *Lobbying the European Union*, Aldershot: Dartmouth 1994.

White House, *A Framework for Global Electronic Commerce*, 1 July 1997.

White House, *Presidential Directive on Electronic Commerce*, memorandum for the heads of executive departments and agencies, 1 July 1997.

White House, Office of the Press Secretary. Joint Statement from Australia and the United States on Electronic Commerce, 20 November 1998.
World Trade Organization, *Electronic Commerce and the Role of the WTO*, Geneva: WTO 1998,
World Trade Organization, *Seminar on Electronic Commerce and Development*, Geneva: WTO 1999.
Zacher, M./Sutton, B., *Governing Global Networks: International Regimes for Transportation and Communications*, Cambridge: Cambridge University Press 1996.

mir *Edition*

Jörg Frehse

International Service Competencies

Strategies for Success in the European Hotel Industry

2002, XXVI, 353 pages, pb., € 59,00 (approx. US $ 59,–)
ISBN 3-409-12349-0

European hotels, which tend to be individual businesses, have a hard time resisting the continued globalization pressure. In order to survive the fierce international competition, Europe's hotel business needs to offer their potential customers an added value that they do not receive from hotel chains. The author shows how European individual hotels can prevail by developing international service competencies.

The book is addressed to lecturers and students of economics, in particular in the field of management and tourism, as well as managers and consultants in the hotel and tourist industry.

Betriebswirtschaftlicher Verlag Dr. Th. Gabler GmbH, Abraham-Lincoln-Str. 46, 65189 Wiesbaden

Steven Globerman

E-Business and Global Sourcing – Inferences from Securities Exchanges

Abstract

- This paper sets out a conceptual model that describes how the configuration of relevant geographic markets might change as electronic "gateways" or portals challenge conventional markets. It then considers the main conceptual inferences against the experience of securities markets. Consideration of empirical evidence suggests that e-business will lead to expanded geographic markets, although the pace and extent of the expansion might be slower and less dramatic, even in the long-run, than early enthusiasts of e-business may have anticipated.

Key Results

- The consolidation of securities exchanges will stop short of the formation of true global portals. Rather, regional securities exchanges will merge or otherwise close down.
- Surviving securities exchanges will become increasingly similar in terms of technological inputs while retaining distinctive features of core competence.

Author

Steven Globerman, Ross Distinguished Professor of Canada-US Business and Economic Relations, College of Business and Economics, Western Washington University, Bellingham, WA, USA.

Steven Globerman

Introduction

A widely acknowledged phenomenon associated with the introduction and spread of e-business practices is the formation of portals for "global" sourcing. In recent years, leading firms in a range of industries have established "group" Web sites to carry out on-line purchasing or sales of products (Globerman 2000). The expectation is that global sourcing though the Internet will enable firms to leverage economies of scale and to greatly reduce transactions costs associated with using "conventional" channels for locating trading partners and organizing the relevant transactions. As a corollary, regional and local markets for the relevant transactions should contract, perhaps even disappear, given the presumed economic advantages of global portal "markets."

The emergence and growth of global portals has potentially wide-ranging and profound implications for corporate and competitive strategies, as well as for public policy. For example, global sourcing through e-business will increasingly obviate the relevance of regionally oriented marketing and distribution activities, and should lead to further centralization of decision-making with respect to various stages of the logistics value-chain. It will also accentuate the benefits of coordinating competition and regulatory policies at a supra-national basis.

Notwithstanding the initial expectations regarding the revolutionary changes that global portals would bring about, the experience, to date, provides grounds for skepticism. Specifically, a substantial number of early e-business Web sites have been closed for lack of sufficient business. These include portals designed to accommodate business-to-business (B to B) e-commerce, the type of e-commerce expected to be characterized by the largest efficiency gains. The relatively slow acceptance of global portals, at least with respect to initial expectations, might merely reflect risk aversion and learning behavior on the part of potential users. Slow initial adoption tends to be characteristic of industrial innovations (Mansfield et al. 1977). On the other hand, it might reflect the limited advantages of global portals compared to purchasing in more localized markets. In particular, it might reflect an initial misperception about the commercial consequences of e-business and, therefore, mistaken perspectives on the extent to which global sourcing will displace more localized industrial purchasing.

The purpose of this paper is to reconsider the potential impact of e-business on global sourcing. Specifically, we discuss the conceptual linkages between e-business and relevant geographic markets. The linkages identify influences that both encourage and discourage more centralized industrial product markets.[1] As a specific case study, we consider the experience, to date, of pan-national stock exchanges. That is, we consider whether and how e-business has contributed to the emergence of global, or near-global portals for the execution of stock market transactions undertaken by brokerage companies.[2] The case study helps explain the relatively slow acceptance of global portals by highlighting how e-business can enhance the competitive advantages of localized providers of industrial products.The paper proceeds as follows. The next section sets out a conceptual framework that describes the general determinants of relevant geographic market size. The third section considers how e-commerce applications might affect the various determinants identified in the preceding section. Section four describes the rise of electronic stock exchanges and evaluates the growth of electronic stock exchanges against the inferences drawn from the conceptual framework. A summary and conclusions is provided in Section five.

Linkages between E-Business and Geographic Markets: A Conceptual Model

In this section we consider the potential for the emergence of global portals to affect the size of relevant geographic markets for products. In this context, global portals may be seen as sites on communication networks through which buyers and sellers can electronically form an agreement concerning the pricing and delivery of a particular good or service and complete the transaction through the delivery of the product or service as contracted. Within this broad definition, the communication networks can be private, quasi-private or public. In practice, the concept of e-business is inextricably linked to the Internet. Hence, for purposes of this discussion, portals for global sourcing of industrial products should be seen as Internet Web sites providing for electronic transacting and, in some cases, electronic delivery of products. Examples of products that can be distributed over the Internet include software, ownership claims to financial securities, and consulting advice.

The presumed relationship between Internet portals and the size of relevant geographic markets derives from the presumed relationship between electronic commerce (e-commerce), more generally, and the geographic scope of competition. For economists, a relevant geographic market is defined as the smallest geographical area in which producers (acting as a monopolist) could implement a profitable price increase. There is a general consensus that e-commerce will result in both the expansion of relevant geographic markets and increased competition within those markets (Malone/Yates/Benjamin 1987, Bakos/Brynjolsson 1993, Kobrin 1995). The two changes are related. Specifically, as e-commerce makes it less costly to identify beneficial transactions across a wider range of potential transactors, it should lead to an increased integration of markets that are currently segmented by high transactions costs across geographical space. Furthermore, geographically larger markets are ordinarily more contestable than smaller markets. Contestable markets are characterized by relatively low costs of entry and exit such that incumbent firms must charge competitive prices even if there are only a small number of such firms (Baumol Panzar/Willig 1988). The Internet might directly increase contestability by enabling entrants to duplicate the "value-creating capabilities" of dominant firms with relatively low sunk cost investments (Kauffman/Subramani/Wood 2000).

In short, to the extent that electronic portals significantly reduce transactions costs that are related to geographical distance, they could lead to a relatively small number of (electronic) markets servicing wide geographical areas. Moreover, to the extent that electronic portals are cheaper than conventional market alternatives, holding distance constant, the resulting lower costs will attract more customers, including those from relatively distant markets. Increased competition within geographical markets should insure that most, if not all, of the cost savings are passed on to consumers. Hence, the emergence and growth of global portals is ultimately related to the impact that the Internet will have on distance-related, as well as non-distance related costs of performing specific transactions, as well as the degree of competition to pass on those cost savings to users.

The basic conceptual relationship can be elaborated upon with the help of Figure 1. The horizontal axis in Figure 1 measures ordinal distance. For convenience, we assume that consumers are distributed in an equi-proportionate fashion along the horizontal axis. The vertical axis measures consumer surplus associated with purchasing the product in question at the location indicated on the horizontal axis. It should be emphasized that all attributes of the product, other than the transaction's location, are implicitly held constant. Consumer surplus, in this case, can be thought of in the conventional way. Specifically, it is the difference between what consumers would be willing to spend to purchase the product

Figure 1. Boundaries of Markets

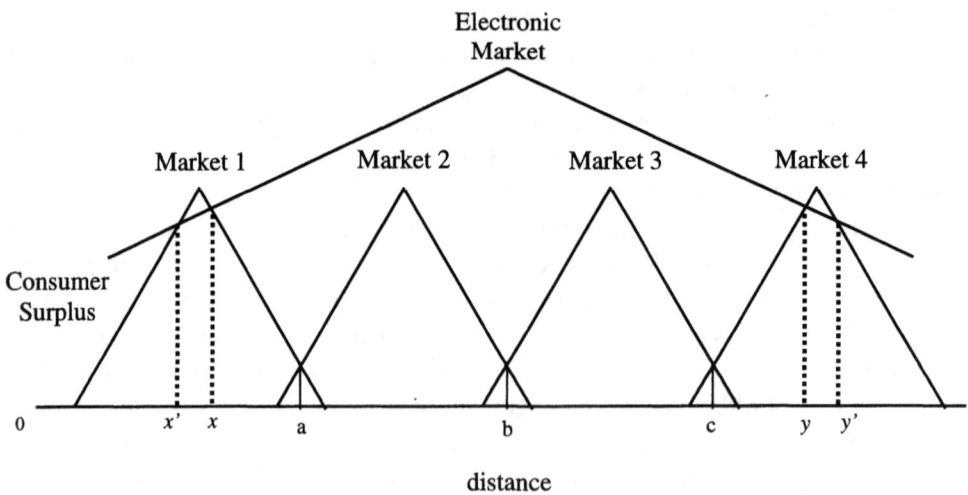

and what they are required to spend by the market. The four geometric peaks shown in Figure 1 therefore represent the surplus that consumers receive from buying a product in the location in which they reside. The cost of buying the product reflects two main factors: the supplier's cost of producing the product and the supplier's cost of "transporting" the product. The lower are either or both of those costs, the larger the surplus that consumers realize assuming competitive pricing.

To elaborate upon Figure 1, the apex of each triangle represents the maximum attainable surplus associated with buying within a given geographical market. Thus, consumers buying from sellers in market 1 realize maximum surplus if they are located on the horizontal axis at the point that is directly below the apex. Consumers located at that point in space will not have to pay transportation costs, although they will pay the same "factory price" as any other buyer. As buyers are located further away from the point directly below the apex, they must incur costs associated with locating the seller, communicating with the seller and taking delivery of the product. The combination of all of these distance-related costs are identified, for convenience, as "transportation costs." As a result, given any factory price, buyers' surplus will decline the further away they are located from the apex. Given four (assumed) groups of sellers concentrated at the four apexes shown in the figure, we have descending surplus values for consumers located at increasing distances away from each apex.

The four triangles represented in Figure 1 define the boundaries of the four relevant geographic markets. Specifically, customers located to the left of point A will find it more advantageous to buy from suppliers located directly below the apex in Market 1. Customers located between points A and B will find it advantageous to purchase from suppliers located directly below the apex labeled Market Two. Similarly, the distance between points B and C marks the boundaries of Market Three, while all customers located to the right of point C will buy from suppliers located below the apex of the triangle marked Market Four.

We now introduce an "electronic portal" into Figure 1. For convenience, we assume that the portal is "located" in the middle of the horizontal axis. We make two other assumptions: 1. The portal is more efficient than any of the conventional sellers represented in the original four triangles. 2. Transportation costs utilizing the portal do not increase as quickly with distance as they do using conventional technology. The import of the efficiency assumption is that the apex for the electronic market should be higher than the apex of any conventional market. That is, holding distance constant, it is assumed to be cheaper to use the electronic market than a conventional market. Therefore, consumer surplus will be higher in the electronic market, other things constant. The import of the transportation cost assumption is that the decrease in surplus from either side of the apex of the electronic market should be less steep than the decrease in surplus from the apex of a conventional market.

These basic assumptions are incorporated into the drawing of the surplus function for an electronic market in Figure 1. The main inference to be drawn is that the electronic market will eliminate the middle two markets (Markets 2 and 3), and substantially reduce the sizes of Markets 1 and 4. In the latter two markets, a relatively small group of consumers around the location directly under each apex will remain loyal to the conventional markets. It can be seen from the diagram that unless the apex of the electronic market is substantially above the apexes of the conventional markets, the latter will not be completely eliminated, even with significantly more gradual declines in the surplus slopes away from the apex of the electronic market. That is, even relatively large differences in efficiency between electronic and conventional markets will likely lead to a consolidation of conventional markets rather than their complete elimination by global portals. Figure 1, as drawn, also shows that modest gains in efficiency using electronic portals may eliminate conventional markets that are relatively "contiguous" to the portals. Thus, the emergence of more efficient electronic markets is more likely to result in the growth of "regional portals" than in the growth of a single truly global portal.

Potential Impacts of E-Business

In this section we consider whether and how serving customers from portals on the Internet might affect the surplus functions of consumers. Specifically, we consider whether such portals should have higher apexes than conventional markets and whether the surplus functions will descend more slowly from the apexes of portals.

Production Efficiency

Obviously, it is very difficult to generalize about how moving value-added activities onto the Internet will affect the basic costs of "producing" the product. Simply put, it will depend very much upon the nature of the underlying production function. For example, to the extent that electronic signals can easily substitute for physical inputs, and to the extent that the former are cheaper than the latter, moving relevant production activities onto the Internet might have substantial cost savings. A number of dramatic examples can be cited in this regard. One company, Micron Computers, reported a productivity gain of a factor of 10 in moving its order placement and execution online. The gain results from the fact that their Web sales people spend, on average, two minutes on the telephone with a customer who has looked at their Web site but 20 minutes with traditional customers (OECD 2000, p.60). Another company, Cisco Systems, claims to have saved over $500 million by moving its customer support activities online (Ibid). Cost-saving claims associated with the use of electronic communication networks are also dramatic. For example, it is estimated that the approximate 3,000 people who work on the floor of the New York Stock Exchange cleared an average of 671,300 trades a day in 1999. By contrast, with only 85 employees, the electronic communication network, Island, cleared an average of 321,007 trades a day in the first half of 2000 (Barber/Odean 2001).

While it is difficult to generalize about how widespread such cost savings might be, the direction of the effect is to make the relevant markets of electronic portals larger at the expense of conventional markets. Relating back to Figure 1, moving specific value-added activities onto the Internet should reduce production costs, on balance, in a variety of industries. This would lead to the apex for the electronic market surplus function increasing relative to those for conventional markets.

The implicit assumption, which might be made explicit at this point, is that sellers in conventional markets do not use the Internet to improve efficiency. Otherwise, the distinction between conventional and electronic markets would quickly become blurred. In practice, this assumption is much too severe. For example, conventional stock markets are increasingly using computer communication systems to carry out transactions with brokerage companies. Significant cost savings are undoubtedly realized from using such systems compared to more traditional telephonic and courier service linkages between brokers and stock exchanges. Nevertheless, there is a distinction between a portal on the Internet and private local or wide-area telecommunications networks. At this point in our discussion, we prefer to make a sharp distinction between electronic and conventional markets. In a later section, when we focus our discussion on stock exchanges, we shall acknowledge that conventional exchanges can lower their costs by selective use of the Internet.

Scale Economies

To the extent that the relevant new technology favors larger-scale production activity, the introduction of that technology should promote a consolidation of local and regional markets. However, unless the new technology is more effectively "exploited" by establishing and operating electronic portals, there is no reason to believe that the expansion of relevant geographic markets will take place by global portals displacing local conventional markets. For example, it could take place through the consolidation of local conventional markets that results in a fewer number of conventional markets serving larger spatial markets. Again, the point is that the relative position of the apexes of the different markets portrayed in

Figure 1 will depend upon the relative abilities of participants in the different types of markets to take advantage of technological change- in this case, using the Internet to carry-out production activities.

Transaction Costs

A broad category of "non-conventional" costs can be identified as "transaction costs". The costs of transacting are essentially comprised of the following components: (1) Search costs: the costs of physically searching for market information related to potential buyers, sellers, product availability, product quality, prices and so forth. (2) Contracting costs: the costs of creating and implementing contractual agreements. (3) Monitoring costs: the costs of ensuring that contractual commitments are satisfied. (4) Adaptation costs: the costs associated with negotiating and implementing changes to agreements over time.[3] These costs can be borne directly by the consumer or by firms serving the consumer. In the latter case, if markets are competitive, transaction costs will ultimately be passed-on to final consumers in the form of higher prices.

It seems obvious that various components of transaction costs will increase with distance between participants in the relevant markets. For example, relevant information about products that is gathered by "word-of-mouth" will be less readily available to individuals at greater distances from other buyers and sellers. As another example, the ability of consumers to "adapt" the terms and conditions of a sale, say by petitioning the seller for altered terms, will be weakened, or will necessitate increased expenditures of time and money, as distance between the buyer and seller increases. Indeed, to the extent that potential redress of original terms includes legal action, and to the extent that increased distance involves crossing national borders, the associated differences in the legal jurisdictions of the buyer and seller may make adaptation costs prohibitive for small-scale market participants. Furthermore, language differences across countries make the contracting process more complex and costly.

Potential Impact of the Internet

It has been argued that the move towards directly transacting on the Internet is broadly driving transaction costs toward zero. A specific claim is that "large and diverse sets of people scattered around the world can now, cheaply and easily, gain near real-time access to the information they need to make smart decisions and coordinate complex activities" (Tapscott 2000, A38). Any conceptual evaluation of this claim requires a closer look at how moving transactions onto Internet portals will affect the various components of transaction costs.

Search Costs

Economists identify a product as a pure "search good" if the important attributes of the product can be readily identified by the consumer prior to purchase. For example, attributes such as price, physical dimension, color and so forth are readily established through simple inquiry or inspection. In this regard, financial securities listed on major stock exchanges have attributes of search goods in that important properties of a security such as price, average trading volume and current dividend yield can be readily and easily determined prior to purchase.

Most discussions of the economic advantages of e-business focus on the reductions in search costs resulting from the increased ease with which information about observable market characteristics such as price, product availability and so forth can be obtained using the Internet. Since the costs of using the Internet are largely distance insensitive, the costs of search on the Internet should be relatively constant as a function of distance, whereas the costs of search through more conventional techniques, such as accessing and reviewing local media and the like, should increase consistently with a participant's distance from the geographical sources of local media outlets. In terms of the components of Figure 1, the slope of the surplus function as it descends from either side of the apex of the global portal should be much flatter than the slopes of the surplus functions as they descend from the apexes of the conventional markets to the extent that claims about the Internet's impact on search costs are appropriate.

Product attributes such as reliability and ease-of -use may not be readily determinable through simple inquiry or inspection. In contrast to search goods, the key attributes of so-called experience goods can only be established by testing or sampling the product. For example, the ease-of-use and reliability of on-line stock brokerages are best established by real-time testing of the product offerings. In some cases, critical attributes of products can only be ascertained with repeated use. For example, the benefits of using any specific financial planner will become much clearer after a period of time. The latter type of product is usually referred to as a "credence good".

While it is widely acknowledged that the Internet is a robust tool for collecting information about search goods, the ability to electronically sample experience goods is expanding the scope for e-business to reduce distance-related costs of acquiring information about those types of goods, as well. As an example, on-line stock trading programs can be downloaded from the seller's Web site and tested by potential buyers. In the case of credence goods, sellers often try to reassure buyers about the claimed attributes of their products by investing in the creation and maintenance of brand names, by offering warranties and customer satisfaction guarantees and so forth. In this regard, it is much less clear how e-business will affect the economics of transacting in credence goods. Traditionally, large accumulated sunk costs in brand names, trademarks and even "bricks and mortar" facilities have been effectively hostages that firms have made available to potential customers in order to engender trust (Klein/Leffler 1981). In the case of e-business, expensive Web sites can serve as potential hostages, although it is unclear whether they can do so as effectively as more traditional sunk cost investments. To the extent that they can, the costs of searching for credence goods may also become relatively insensitive to distance.

Other Transaction Cost Components

In summary, e-business applications should lower distance-related search costs. However, it is less obvious how e-business will affect other components of transaction costs. One argument is that the widespread adoption of standardized electronic contracts will lower the average costs of "simple" contracting, especially for business-to-business transactions, since a repetitive activity with relatively high variable costs will be replaced by an activity with relatively high "once-and-for-all" fixed and sunk costs but relatively low variable costs. In fact, this is more a claim for economies of scale associated with e-business rather than an argument about the distance sensitivity of contracting costs under e-business versus conventional market techniques.

The practical relevance of the claim that the Internet will facilitate a higher degree of standardized contracting is uncertain. For one thing, there are unresolved legal issues surrounding the enforceability of e-commerce agreements, although recent legislation affirming that electronic signatures are as binding as non-electronic signatures on legal contracts points towards a resolution of those issues. For another, it is unclear that transactions between parties, including those who regularly do business together, are sufficiently standardized as to obviate the need for contract modifications on an ongoing and, perhaps, unpredictable basis. This caveat is especially relevant for international transactions where differences in legal regimes, contractual customs and so forth may oblige parties to enter into multiple agreements with a resulting loss of opportunities to standardize contracts and other agreements.

To the extent that the perceived risks of opportunistic behavior are no lower for e-business activities than for conventional commercial activities, electronic agreements may need to be at least as complex and as frequently adapted over time as non-electronic agreements. In this case, the use of Internet portals may have little direct impact on the costs of creating and enforcing commercial agreements. On the other hand, to the extent that the substitution of electronic portals for conventional markets significantly expands the relevant geographic markets for products, buyers and sellers of those products should experience lower costs associated with switching transactions partners. Lower switching costs, in turn, should reduce incentives for individual market participants to act opportunistically, all other things constant, which, in turn, should reduce the costs of establishing, maintaining and enforcing contracts. Again, the reduction in relevant costs should be greater for participants located further from centers of conventional markets, since any increase in competition should be greater at the periphery of conventional markets.

Summary

In summary, the spread of e-business, with electronic portals effectively functioning as markets, should reduce distance-related transaction costs. All other things constant, this should expand relevant geographic markets and lead to the substitution of portals serving relatively broad spatial markets for more localized conventional markets. The magnitude of this phenomenon clearly depends upon the impact of e-commerce on distance-related transaction costs, and this could vary across product markets. On the other hand, it is less clear that the adoption of electronic portals will reduce non-distance related costs, such as production costs, relative to similar costs incurred through more conventional ways of carrying-out the relevant value-chain activities. In particular, in many cases it may not be possible to standardize the underlying electronic transactions so as to leverage latent economies of scale compared to conventional production techniques. In other cases, participants in conventional markets may also be able to exploit cost-saving benefits of computer technology so as to offset any cost-saving advantages that would be otherwise realized by transacting through Internet portals.

The conceptual framework described in this section leads to a prediction that e-business will result in an expansion of relevant geographic markets. It is much less supportive of a prediction that truly global portals will completely displace conventional markets in many, if indeed any, activities. To the extent that distance-related costs are reduced by e-business, there should be some consolidation of regional and local markets with regional Internet portals hosting the displaced transactions. However, unless e-business also reduces non-distance related costs substantially, transactions carried out close to the centers of major conventional markets may not migrate to Internet portals.

In the next section of the paper, we consider the early historical experience of electronic stock markets. In particular, we review this experience with a view towards assessing whether and to what extent it supports the broad inferences about global portals that are drawn from our conceptual framework.

Electronic Stock Exchanges

Over the past few years, electronic communications networks (ECNs) have emerged as potential alternatives to conventional equity trading arrangements. An

ECN is an automated trading system that disseminates orders to third parties and dealers and can execute such orders within the network itself. ECNs typically do not serve individual investors, but instead focus on brokers and institutional investors. The latter, in turn, are agents who buy and sell securities for the ultimate benefit of customers or shareholders, although brokerage companies are also major shareholders in a number of ECNs. The latter therefore function as exchanges in which buyers and sellers of securities transact with each other. However, they are not regulated as securities exchanges, as are conventional stock exchanges such as the New York Stock Exchange. Rather, they are regulated as broker-dealers. The regulatory status of ECNs is a potentially important issue in the competition between ECNs and conventional security exchanges, and more will be said about this issue in a later section.[4]

ECNs function by electronically posting orders to buy or sell specific quantities of a stock at a specific price. These orders are received from clients, and the computer systems automatically complete transactions internally when they find appropriate matches between buyers and sellers. When internal matches are not found, the ECNs post the orders on the National Association of Securities Dealers Automated Quote (Nasdaq) system as soon as an order becomes the network's best bid or offer for a stock (McAndrews/Stefanadis 2000).

Analogies to Internet Portals

It should be noted explicitly that ECNs are not Internet portals in the conventional sense, in that they are private computer-communication networks rather than nodes of the public Internet. However, the analogy to Internet portals is apt in comparison to the traditional market center approaches to trading securities. The New York Stock Exchange (NYSE) is the largest traditional stock exchange center. Trading on the NYSE is structured around a specialist. For each stock, one specialist has an exclusive franchise. As an agent, the specialist matches buy and sell orders and handles limit orders placed with brokers. As a dealer, the specialist sometimes posts his or her own price quotes on the market and trades from his or her own liquidity. The NYSE has an electronic transmission system through which member firms can place small market orders. However, orders are executed manually by the specialist.

The Over-the-Counter Market (OTC) also uses a specialist system to execute trading in stocks not listed on an exchange. The difference between the NYSE and the OTC is that the latter uses multiple specialists for individual stocks. For the OTC, brokers can route orders to specialist dealers by telephone or computer network. However, the dealer is responsible for execution. As in the case of the NYSE, the dealer possesses proprietary information about unexecuted limit orders which puts the dealer at a major advantage to non-dealer participants

(McAndrews/Stefanadis 2000, p. 2). Unlike the US, with its system of market makers and specialists, European bourses rely upon electronic order-matching systems.

The analogy between ECNs and Internet portals is suggested primarily by the fact that price quotations and limit orders must be displayed publicly by ECNs on the Nasdaq public exchange. This regulatory requirement effectively links ECNs with the broader public market for securities trading by allowing counter-parties to transact indirectly with the ECN. Specifically, regulatory requirements have the practical effect of requiring Nasdaq dealers to match ECN bid or ask prices if the latter are more favorable than the dealer's quotations. As a consequence, even though most ECN trading ultimately is linked to trading over the counter on the Nasdaq, the prices of such trades arguably reflect broader public participation than trades executed through the traditional dealer-specialist route.

The theoretical potential exists for the ultimate interconnection of all conventional securities markets to ECNs though arrangements similar to those described above for the Nasdaq. With an evolution of the trading system to a relatively small number of relatively large ECNs, the analogy to a set of electronic portals carrying-out securities trading transactions would become closer. Indeed, the theoretical "limiting case" would be a small number of ECNs, indeed even a single ECN, that carry-out all securities trading at the wholesale level, thereby completely displacing the conventional dealer-specialist arrangements. In fact, initiatives undertaken by the Nasdaq in recent years can be seen as an attempt to set such an evolution of market structure in motion. The resulting experience therefore is potentially instructive of the linkages between spatial markets and e-business more broadly defined.

Organizational Changes by Securities Exchanges

ECNs rely primarily upon the quick routing and executing of trades, as well as set commissions per trade, to generate competitive advantages over conventional exchanges. To date, ECNs have done relatively little business directly linking buyers and sellers of securities while bypassing specialists and dealers on established stock exchanges. However, they have grown to account for almost half of the volume in trading of Nasdaq Stock Market-listed securities as of year-end 2000 (Kelly 2001b).[5] The Nasdaq, in turn, has sought to establish outposts in Europe and Asia that would list fledgling overseas companies and then link those overseas market operations with Nasdaq's flagship US market. Specifically, Nasdaq Japan operates as a section of the Osaka Securities Exchange. Nasdaq also acquired Easdaq, a Brussels-based pan-European stock market.[6] Nasdaq plans to link its US, European and Japanese operations with a common trade-clearing and settlement system within a few years. Hence, Nasdaq's electronic trading platform is arguably emerging as the most likely candidate for a global securities exchange portal.

Nasdaq Japan and Easdaq have apparently generated relatively little trading volume, to date, and have also failed to attract many stock market listings. Various reasons have been offered. One is that efforts to link local stock exchanges into a pan-national trade clearing and settlement system are hampered by differences in cross-border regulatory and reporting procedures. Such differences substantially increase costs associated with processing trades across national boundaries and can make integration prohibitively costly.[7] In this regard, talks have been initiated by organizations from the US, Europe, Asia and Latin America that do clearance and settlement of securities transactions to see if better international cooperation in those activities can be realized (Garten 2001). A second reason is that larger companies are reluctant to list on new Nasdaq exchanges given long-standing commercial and "personal" ties between company executives and officials of established local stock exchanges. The failure to attract new listings limits the growth of trading volume that, in turn, attenuates the ability of the new exchanges to exploit economies of scale associated with their technology platforms. In this regard, new exchanges face something of a "Catch 22" problem. Companies are reluctant to list their large capitalization stock on exchanges unless those exchanges can provide substantial liquidity to market participants. On the other hand, without a roster of listed large capitalization stocks, it may be difficult to generate customer interest in new exchanges.

A third reason with, perhaps, the most enduring significance is the response of conventional stock exchanges to the initiatives of new electronic trading platforms. In particular, conventional exchanges have sought to reduce the costs of trading and listing for their clients. One way has been through consolidations involving mergers and alliances to gain the advantages of economies of scale. Figure 2 provides a partial list of recently announced international mergers, joint ventures and other types of alliances involving national and regional stock exchanges. The industrial reorganization appears to be motivated by several objectives: 1) the facilitation of "after-hours" trading; 2) the sharing of costs of trading and settlement technology platforms; 3) the promotion of specialized listings and cross-listings of securities (Globerman/Roehl/Standifird 2001). Disagreement about precisely how to achieve those objectives can limit the pace of this consolidation. A case in point is the failed merger between the London Stock Exchange and the Deutsche Bourse. However, the trend towards consolidation seems firmly in place.

A second set of initiatives by conventional stock markets relates to the adoption of new technology in order to lower costs and increase transacting speed. For example, the NYSE has updated its electronic order system designed to transmit market orders for share blocks of stock from member firms to the trading posts on the exchange floor (Westland/Clark 2000). The updates have vastly expanded

Figure 2. Mergers and Alliances Between Stock Exchanges

Exchanges	Features	Announcement Date
Singapore Exchange & Australian Stock Exchange (merger)	Link Trading and Settlement Systems	June 2000
Global Equity Market*	Pass Order Books across Time Zones	June 2000
Deutsche Boerse & London Stock Exchange (merger)	Share Trading and Regulatory Systems; Specialization by Security Type	April 2000
Deutsche Boerse & Market XT (joint venture)	Create an European Broker/Dealer Giving US Investors Access to European Blue Chips via Germany	April 2000
Nasdaq & Quebec Government (joint venture)	Co-Listing Agreement	April 2000
Nasdaq & Stock Exchange of Hong Kong	Trading Nasdaq Stocks in HK	June 2000
Copenhagen Stock Exchange & Stockholm Stock Exchange (Alliance)	Integrated Trading, Clearing & Settlement Systems	January 1998
Swiss Exchange & Tradepoint Financial Network	Integrated Settlement Systems	May 2000
London Stock Exchange & Deutsche Boerse	Integrated Trading, Clearing & Settlement Systems	Not Completed

* A venture involving the New York, Toronto, Tokyo and Hong Kong exchanges and bourses in Paris, Amsterdam, Australia, Brussels, Mexico and Brazil.

Source: Newspaper Reports

the capacity of the system to handle orders without delay. Conventional stock exchanges have also encouraged cross listing of shares to facilitate "24-hour" trading in specific stocks, thereby promoting a "virtual" global market for the shares of specific companies.

Notwithstanding the technological innovations undertaken by established conventional exchanges, swifter trade execution remains an advantage of ECNs. For example, the average turnaround time for an ECN-executed order is two to three seconds compared with twenty-two seconds for an order processed though the

NYSE (Smith/Ip/Gasparino 1999). Furthermore, emerging software developments promise to facilitate a much faster scanning of liquidity and price offerings across markets to allow execution of an order at the best price anywhere at a moment in time (Schmerken 1999). This software can serve to effectively link different ECNs or other markets such that brokers can obtain the best terms-of-trade for their clients wherever a stock is traded. The potential exists for such software to move markets towards *de facto* global integration if not *de jure* integration. Indeed, the interest being shown by conventional exchanges in such software suggests the possibility that such integration might occur without a displacement of the conventional exchanges by ECNs.

In summary, the structural changes in securities markets associated with new computer communication technologies are broadly consistent with the conceptual model developed in Section 2. Specifically, by lowering costs associated with "producing" securities transactions, non-conventional markets threaten to take customers away from conventional markets. Notwithstanding regulatory and other barriers to the ability of individual ECNs to carry out transactions across national boundaries, the emergence of ECNs has led to the expansion of relevant geographic markets in securities trading at the wholesale level. To date, this has largely occurred as a result of mergers and joint ventures among conventional, and, more often, regional stock exchanges in response to the competitive threat of ECNs. Conventional exchanges have also responded to the threat of ECNs by utilizing new technology to improve their own efficiency, and by undertaking initiatives, such as increased cross-exchange listing of securities, that have the practical effect of increasing the spatial distance over which conventional stock trading transactions occur.

Future Outlook

There is every reason to expect that technological changes in communications will perpetuate the market pressures generated by the growth of ECNs. As noted above, the emergence of "pricing engines" will improve the ability of brokers to identify the best buy or sell price for a security across different markets. One can therefore anticipate the development of interconnected ECNs, or interconnected conventional markets, in which a technology platform, perhaps maintained in a central location, routes buy and sell orders throughout the network (Schmerken 1999). With the reduction, if not complete elimination, of regulatory and related idiosyncrasies surrounding national, and even regional stock markets, major further contractions can be anticipated in the number of conventional exchanges. The remaining exchanges will be larger and will serve a larger geographical area. At the same time, the desire for liquidity should lead to a contraction in the number of ECNs, as well.

It is unlikely, however, that an evolution towards truly global portals will occur. In particular, the ability of local specialists to provide services, such as supplying liquidity through their own intervention in the market, may be difficult to duplicate in a purely electronic market. Moreover, it is unlikely that any single exchange, whether purely electronic or not, will satisfy all market participants given the different emphasis placed on service attributes such as speed of execution, quality of information about listed securities, liquidity and so forth. Indeed, ECNs continue to differ in the extent to which they emphasize matching buying and selling orders internally versus acting as "order routers" to other exchanges (Ceron 2001).

The reputations of established conventional exchanges for honest and "fair" dealing may also mitigate the technological advantages enjoyed by ECNs. The reputations of securities exchanges are, in turn, often linked to investor perceptions that those exchanges are "soundly" and effectively regulated. On this point, there is evidence that companies are rewarded, through lower capital costs, by listing their securities on exchanges with reputations for being effectively regulated (Standifird/Weinstein 2002). As noted above, the ability to attract new listings from major companies is an important factor conditioning the growth of new securities exchanges. In this regard, the current regulatory status of ECNs might discourage such new listings. Currently, most ECNs are regulated as broker-dealers. As such, they are subject to oversight by self-regulatory organizations that themselves operate exchanges. In particular, ECNs are not subject to the same surveillance and examination procedures as conventional securities exchanges. Nor do they have an obligation to ensure that they have sufficient capacity to handle trading demand as do conventional securities exchanges.

The Securities and Exchange Commission (1997) has signaled its intent to alter domestic securities market regulations to acknowledge the changes that have been brought about by the Internet. It is likely that the ensuing changes will move the regulation of ECNs closer to that of traditional stock exchange markets. In doing so, the regulator will almost certainly inflict higher costs on ECN operations, while, at the same time, it's actions will probably enhance the perception of market participants that ECNs operate as reliable and honest market clearing platforms. It is unclear whether the net result will be to improve or diminish the relative competitive position of ECNs.

It is less clear how the regulator will address foreign securities market activities in the United States. One possibility is that traditional exchange regulation will be applied to foreign securities markets that seek to do business in the United States. Another is that the US regulator will rely solely on home country regulation of the foreign markets. Clearly, the growth of international securities exchanges will be promoted by the harmonization of national regulations, especially if the level of harmonization does not inflict undue costs upon newer pan-national markets. At the same time, investors have a strong "home country bias."

Specifically, investors, including institutional investors, have a propensity to invest in local stocks and securities markets (Tse 1999). One possible explanation of this propensity is that information about specific corporate securities is more readily available in regional and local markets, especially general information that is unlikely to be published (Coval/Moskowitz 1999). The persistence of a home country bias on the part of investors reduces the appeal of having low-cost access to "foreign" securities markets, especially if the latter have disproportionately large listings of foreign corporate securities.

Concluding Comments

A broad inference that might be drawn from the securities exchange experience is as follows: e-business unambiguously contributes to the expansion of relevant geographic markets. However, the speed and extent to which spatial markets expand are conditioned by a host of factors. Some, such as government regulations and legislation, may be largely unrelated to technological and other developments driving the expansion of e-business, although the relevant new technologies may make it increasingly difficult for governments to use regulations to segment local markets from international competition. Others will be related to the competitive responses of participants in conventional markets including the latters' willingness and ability to utilize new technology to lower their costs of production. Technological change, itself, will be important. In particular, the ability of technology to allow participants in a market, wherever they are located, to transact at the same speed as other participants is critical to building market liquidity.

Against the background of these factors to date, the securities exchange experience suggests that the emergence of truly global portals is unlikely, although there is likely to be a significant consolidation of existing markets. The consolidation could be a fairly lengthy process and will largely occur at the regional level, e.g. within Europe and North America. In short, the Internet should lead to smaller numbers of markets within major regions of the world with a resulting increase in cross-border trade within those regions. Furthermore, the widespread adoption of new communications technologies by operators of traditional exchange markets will increasingly blur the distinction between electronic markets and traditional markets.

As noted above, ECNs are interesting cases to study in that electronic trading of securities has been at the forefront of the e-business phenomenon, at least at the retail level, and the fundamental importance of speed of information exchange and transaction execution in securities trading makes the adoption of new technology of great relevance to participants in that industry.[8] Hence, it might be argued that the consolidation of geographic markets in other industries, along with the emergence of cross-border electronic markets, will proceed at a significantly slower pace than in the securities industry. Nevertheless, managers who ignore the inevitable technological forces driving the closer integration of geographical markets are placing their organizations in serious competitive jeopardy.

Endnotes

1 We focus on industrial product markets, since they are more likely than retail consumer markets to become more centralized. For example, retail consumers face much higher information and transportation costs related to distance than do industrial customers. Certainly, if global portals do not "catch on" with industrial customers, they will be a much harder "sell" to retail customers, notwithstanding E-Bay's apparent success.

2 A focus on brokerage companies, rather than brokerage customers, is consistent with an examination of industrial product markets rather than retail markets. For an analysis of the impact of e-commerce on the retail brokerage sector, see Globerman, Roehl and Standifird (2001). For a broader examination of the impact of the Internet on investor behavior, see Barber and Odean (2001).

3 This categorization of transaction costs is discussed in Wigand (1997). An important component of search activity is the verification of the claimed attributes of products. Where it is difficult for producers to validate their product claims, markets may be characterized by a "lemons" problem, and reliable producers may be driven from the market. For a discussion of this phenomenon on the Internet, see Lu (1998).

4 Along with ECNs, there are other types of alternative trading systems. For example, crossing networks temporarily aggregate liquidity by matching submitted bids and offers for securities at distinct times of the day. The latter are not regulated, either as brokers or security exchanges, and they process a relatively small share of total securities transactions. For a description of the various alternative trading systems, see Barber and Odean (2001).

5 The oldest and historically the largest electronic stock-trading platform is operated by the Instinet Group. The latter accounted for almost 30% of ECN-generated Nasdaq trading volume in 2000. The next largest 5 ECNs accounted for essentially all of the rest of ECN-generated Nasdaq trading volume (Kelly 2001a, C1). It was recently reported that Island ECN has overtaken Instinet as the top electronic stock trader by market share (Kelly/Frank 2002). Moreover, a planned merger between two other ECNs (Archipelago and Redibook) will leave the merged entity with a larger market share than Instinet (Kelly 2001b).

6 These initiatives are discussed in "Nasdaq's Drive to Build Global Exchange Hits Some Major Potholes", *The Wall Street Journal*, June 25, 2001, A1, A6. Two recently established joint ventures between NASDAQ and regional stock markets outside the United States are identified in Figure 2 along with a number of announced mergers between established stock exchanges. The relevance of the merger trend will be discussed in a later section. It might be noted that several start-ups have also recently announced that they will launch pan – European exchanges. See Ascarelli (2001).

7 See "Taking one's Easdaq," *The Economist*, February 3, 2001, p.77. To some extent, computer technology is driving down costs of settlement procedures by automating manual clearance procedures and by assisting brokers to compare costs of different suppliers of clearance and settlement services and bypass the least efficient suppliers. See "the hunt for liquidity," *The Economist*, July 28, p.65.

8 Ultimately, changes at the exchange level will also be influenced by the demand for electronic trading at the retail level, since it is the customer's demand for rapid execution at the best possible price that will drive demand for fast and liquid electronic markets. For an assessment of the outlook for Web-based stock trading at the retail level, see McNamee (2001).

References

Ascarelli, S., Nasdaq's European Exchange Will Move to a New Electronic Trading System, *The Wall Street Journal*, May 11, 2001, p. C14.
Bakos, J. Y./Brynjolfsson, E., From Vendors to Partners: Information Technology and Incomplete Contracts in Buyer-Supplier Relationships, *Journal of Organizational Computing*, 3, 3, 1993, pp. 301–328.
Barber, B. M./Odean, T., The Internet and the Investor, *Journal of Economic Perspectives*, 15 1, 2001, pp. 41–54.
Baumol,W. J., Panzar J. C./Willig, R. D., *Contestable Markets and the Theory of Industry Structure*, New York: Harcourt Brace Jovanovich 1982.
Ceron, G. F., Stock-Trading Networks Differ More as They Age, *The Wall Street Journal*, March 20, 2001, p. B9D.
Coval, J. D./Moskowitz, T. J., Home Bias at Home: Local Equity Preference in Domestic Portfolios, *The Journal of Finance*, 54, 6, 1999, pp. 2045–2073.
Garten, J. E., Global Stock Trading Needs Fixing – and Fast, *Business Week*, January 29, 2001, p. 24.
Globerman, S., Electronic Commerce and Productivity Growth: Defining and Assessing the Linkages, Western Washington University, mimeo 2000.
Globerman, S., Roehl, T.W/Standifird, S., Globalization and Electronic Commerce: Inference from Retail Brokering, *Journal of International Business Studies*, 32 4, 2001, pp. 749–768.
Kauffman, R. J., M. Subramani/Wood, C., Analyzing Information Intermediaries in Electronic Brokerage, University of Minnesota Information System Research Center Working Paper Series, 2000, pp. 2000–2010.
Kelly, K., Instinet IPO Is Shaping Up as a Rare Hit, *The Wall Street Journal*, May 18, 2001a, p. C1.
Kelly, K., Archipelago and Redibook Agree to Merge Into One ECN Entity, *The Wall Street Journal*, November 29, 2001b, p. C18.
Kelly, K./Frank, R., Instinet's, CEO Quits as Reuters Weighs Options, *The Wall Street Journal*, April 10, 2002, p. C1.
Klein, B./Leffler, K., The Role of Market Forces in Assuring Contractual Performance, *Journal of Political Economy*, 89, 1981, pp. 615–641.
Kobrin, S. J., Regional Integration in a Globally Networked Economy, *Transnational Corporations*, 4, 2, 1995, pp. 15–33.
Lu, J., Lemons in Cyberspace: A Call for Middlemen, in Bohlin, E./Levin, S. L. (eds.), *Telecommunications Transformation: Technology, Strategy and Policy*, Amsterdam: IOS Press 1998, pp. 235–253.
Malone, T. W., Yates, J./Benjamin, R. I., Electronic Markets and Electronic Hierarchies: Effects of Information Technology on Market Structure and Corporate Strategies, *Communications of the ACM*, 30, 6, 1987, pp. 484–497.
Mansfield, E., Rapoport, J., Romeo, A.,Villani, E., Wagner, S./Husic, F., *The Production and Application of New Industrial Technology*, New York: W. W. Norton & Company, Inc. 1977.
McAndrews, J./Stefanadis, C., The Emergence of Electronic Communications Networks in the U. S. Equity Markets, *Federal Reserve Bank of New York Current Issues*, 6, 12, 2000, pp. 1–6.
McNamee, M., Winning Back the Web Weary, *Business Week*, May 28, 2001, pp. 98–104.
OECD, *The Economic and Social Impacts of Electronic Commerce: Preliminary Findings and Research Agenda*, Paris: OECD, mimeo 2000.

Schmerken, I., ECN Portals Serve Up a Menu of Appetizing Choices, *Wall Street & Technology*, November 1999, pp. 10–14.

Securities and Exchange Commission, 17 CFR Part 240, Release 34–38672, *Regulation of Exchanges*, Washington, D. C.: mimeo 1997.

Smith, R., Ip, G./Gasparino, C., Bitter Rivals Jointly Seek Major Changes in the Markets, *The Wall Street Journal*, October 1, 1999, p. C2.

Standifird, S./Weinstein, M., Establishing Legitimacy in Emerging Markets: An Empirical Comparison of the Warsaw, Budapest and Prague Stock Exchanges, *Journal of Comparative Policy Analysis: Research and Practice*, 4, 1, 2002, pp. 143–163.

Tapscott, D., Virtual Webs Will Revolutionize Business, *The Wall Street Journal*, April 24, 2000, p. A38.

Tse, Y., Round-the-Clock Market Efficiency and Home Bias: Evidence from the International Japanese Government Bond Futures Markets, *Journal of Banking and Finance*, 23, 12, 1999, pp. 1831–1860.

Westland, J. C./Clark T. H. K., *Global Electronic Commerce: Theory and Case Studies*, Cambridge, Mass.: The MIT Press 2000.

Wigand, R., Electronic Commerce: Definitions, Theory and Context, *The Information Society*, 13, 1997, pp. 1–16.

mir *Edition*

Tobias Specker

Postmerger – Management in den ost- und mitteleuropäischen Transformationsstaaten

2002, XX, 431 pages, Br., € 64,– (approx. US $ 58.–)
ISBN 3-409-12010-6

Since the beginning of the transformation process in the Middle and Eastern European countries, German companies have put a special emphasis on entering these markets via corporate acquisitions. Tobias Specker analyses the critical issue of postmerger management with a specific focus on the particular transformation context. His theoretical reflections are supported by results of an explorative study of various German companies.

The book is addressed to lecturers and students of international management. Consultants and managers will also receive valuable information.

Betriebswirtschaftlicher Verlag Dr. Th. Gabler GmbH, Abraham-Lincoln-Str. 46, 65189 Wiesbaden

Denice E. Welch/Verner Worm/Marilyn Fenwick

Are Virtual International Assignments Feasible?

Abstract

- Some international companies are using advanced communication and information technology to manage virtually, rather than sending a traditional expatriate into the foreign location.
- This article explores the feasibility of using virtual assignments as a replacement for the traditional expatriate international posting.

Key Results

- A schema is presented to illustrate elements of a virtual assignee's work relationship.
- The virtual assignment is a viable option but is unlikely to replace traditional expatriate assignments.

Authors

Denice E. Welch, Professor of International Management, Mt Eliza Business School, Melbourne, and the University of Queensland, Australia.
Verner Worm, Associate Professor of International Management, Asia Research Center, Department of International Economics and Management, Copenhagen Business School, Copenhagen, Denmark.
Marilyn Fenwick, Senior Lecturer, Department of Management, Faculty of Business and Economics, Monash University, Melbourne, Australia.

Denice E. Welch/Verner Worm/Marilyn Fenwick

Introduction

Foreign operations place particular demands on management due to the inherent economic and political risks involved in operating in multiple markets. Of course, these management demands vary across industries, firm size and geographical spread, and mode of foreign operation utilized. However, there are generic management concerns that internationalising firms face, as indicated in the burgeoning volume of scientific literature on international management. Within this work, there is general recognition that the need for effective performance monitoring and control of global activities is of critical importance. A common response has been to use staff transfers as a control mechanism (Edström/Galbraith 1977, Ondrack 1985, Fenwick/ De Cieri/Welch 1999). This approach allows the internationalising firm to fill key positions in foreign units with expatriates, whether from headquarters or from other subsidiaries. The challenge is that, as activities spread globally, the demand for internationally mobile staff becomes more acute and may become a barrier to further globalisation (Novicevic/Harvey 2001, Harris 1999, Latta 1999, Tung 1998, Welch 1994).

In this article, we explore the feasibility of using a "virtual" assignment as a replacement to the traditional expatriate international posting as a way of meeting the staffing challenge. The virtual assignment has been defined as a situation where "an employee does not relocate to a host location, but has international responsibilities for a part of the organisation in another country which they manage from the home country" (PricewaterhouseCoopers 2000, p. 31). It is an appointment to a specific, defined role in a foreign operation, for a specific period of time. The difference is that the traditional expatriate assignment requires the person to relocate to the foreign work setting. Companies therefore require persons/family units that are internationally mobile. However, demographic changes such as the increasing number of dual career couples, as more females seek equal opportunities to advance their international careers, are affecting the available pool of potential, mobile, expatriates. The traditional family unit – a male breadwinner supported by a spouse who has either no career outside the family work environment, or has a part-time attachment to the paid workforce – is declining. Compensation for the loss of income of the accompanying spouse/partner has become an issue adding to the expense of using traditional expatriate postings. Therefore, increasing staff immobility and cost constraints appear to be important drivers in the search for alternative ways of handling international staffing requirements than through the traditional form of expatriation. Recent Danish and Australian research into International Human Resource Management (IHRM) trends (conducted by two of the authors of this article) highlights this. For example, Danish line managers reported that, when potential expatriates were approached, half of them refused to accept an international assignment.

As barriers to staff mobility increase, international companies are utilising other staffing options to reduce their reliance on traditional expatriate assignments. One alternative has been to try to localise as soon as practicable – the expatriate trains his/her replacement. For example, ABB China has made localisation a business goal. To achieve this, profit and market share targets are linked to expatriates' annual monetary bonuses, determined by the speed by which they have successfully developed a local who can take over expatriates' roles. As a result ABB has comparatively the lowest number of expatriates with a ratio of 1:100 among seven major European MNCs in China. By focusing so strongly on localisation, they were able to reduce cost considerably because an expatriate's remuneration including allowances per year is around ten times more than the typical salary of a local manager (Worm/Selmer/de Leon 2001).

Another option is to select from the many forms of what has been termed non-standard assignments – that is, other than the traditional expatriate assignment. These include: *short term assignments* (transfers abroad that range in duration from longer than a business trip, but shorter than the typical long term assignment); *commuter assignments* (special arrangements where the person concerned commutes from the home country on a weekly or bi-weekly basis to the place of work in another country); *rotational assignments* (employees commute from the home country to a place of work in another country for a short set period followed by a holiday in the home country – used on oil rigs for example); and *contractual assignments* (used in situations where employees with specific skills vital to an international project are assigned for a limited duration of six to twelve months).

The consulting firm, PricewaterhouseCoopers conducts periodic surveys of international firms operating in Europe. Its 1997/1998 survey identified a trend towards increased use of non-standard international assignments, and this trend was confirmed in its follow-up survey in 2000. The PricewaterhouseCoopers surveys also identified the emergence of the growing use of the so-called '*virtual assignment*'. The 2000 survey found that 28% of respondent firms anticipated an increasing use of virtual assignments, compared with 17% in the 1997/1998 survey. 65% of respondents who use virtual assignments reported having seen an increase in the number of virtual assignments used by their company and the same proportion indicated an expected increase in the next two years. The survey data indicates that the importance and use of virtual assignments has increased most significantly, in relative terms, compared with the other types of non-standard and the traditional expatriate assignments.

Given the above, this article now examines the virtual assignment as an alternative form of international staffing. We seek to provide a window on this alternative through the exploration of the virtual assignment concept. What are the key issues in using a virtual rather than the traditional form of expatriate assignment, considering that it involves managing discrete activities, involving foreign-based work groups, remote from the actual location? What are the implications of relying on telecommunication and information technology such as telephone, e-mail and video conferencing as a *substitute for actual physical presence* in the foreign work context? Is it a long-term, viable international staffing option that will be an effective replacement for the traditional expatriate assignment or just a variant of the traditional expatriate assignment, its use influenced by the hype that has surrounded the Internet and E Commerce? These questions form the starting point for our examination of the virtual assignment as a non-standard form of staffing foreign operations and activities. While the central focus is the nature of the virtual assignment, we also attempt to delineate aspects that may affect the working relationship between the Virtual Assignee and the Virtual Workgroup involved in the host location. Through iteration with the relevant extant literature, and drawing upon the limited empirical work in this area, a schematic portrayal of factors (Figure 1) influencing virtual assignees and their work groups is presented and discussed.

There is a substantial body of research into the management of expatriates in traditional, longer-term assignments (for a review of this literature, see for example, Dowling/Welch/Schuler 1999). However, while non-standard assignments have long been used in conjunction with, or instead of, traditional expatriate assignments, this has yet to translate into a comparable body of academic inquiry. Consequently, there has been a dearth of research into the international management issues, particularly human resource implications, of using other than traditional expatriate assignments. This article seeks to assist in redressing this imbalance by focusing on one form of non-standard assignment – the virtual assignment.

Confirming Trends

As mentioned above, the use of virtual and other forms of non-standard international assignments appear to be increasing. In this section, we draw out issues that emerged from our Australian and Danish studies that were conducted in 2000 and 2001 to identify trends in multinational staffing approaches regarding non-standard assignments. These studies have formed the basis for on–going empirical investigations into the virtual assignment. Both studies used in-depth interviews that were tape recorded with the interviewees' permission, transcribed verbatim, and subsequently manually content-analysed (within-case and across case) following the pattern-matching approach outlined by Miles and Huberman (1994).

An Australian Perspective

Five expert informants were interviewed in order to explore staffing trends and whether or not virtual assignments featured in their lines of sight. Consistent with a Delphi-type research design, four consultants and one senior human resource practitioner were selected for interview on the basis that such professionals have been found to be reliable expert informants (Chen/Farh/MacMillan 1993). The five experts were: the Managing Director of an Australian–owned and operated international relocation consultancy; a senior consultant with a large multinational consultancy specialising in reward and recognition practices; a senior consultant in international assignment management with a large multinational management consultancy; the Human Resources Director with a multinational trading company; and, a principal in the Human Resources and Remuneration consulting division of a worldwide consulting firm.

The changing demographics of those undertaking international assignments, and an increase in project-based international assignments of shorter duration (such as those found in the PricewaterhouseCoopers surveys) were the main themes that emerged from the interviews. The following comment is illustrative:

> *There's definitely a shift for younger people to go on assignment. Rather than having* [international assignees who] *go in as country heads at the age of 42 . . . I would say that 60–70% of the people that we move around are under 37.*

In the opinions of the expert informants, there were indications this shift might be more characteristic of information and high technology industries in particular. The consultants indicated that project-based international assignments of shorter duration were increasingly a feature across the banking, mining, information technology and trading organisations for example. For instance, a relocation consultant commented:

> *We started the business* [over a decade] *ago and the average length of assignment then would have been three years . . . I'd say the average length of assignment now is 18 months.*

Interviewees also considered that international assignments, particularly the non-standard types, were increasingly being undertaken by all management levels, including supervisory and line management levels. The use of 'virtual teams' appears to be increasing, according to all the experts interviewed, driven by the advent of intra- and inter- net communications and advances in teleconferencing technology. For example,

I would say we are using a lot more virtual teams and electronic communication to reduce expensive and risky expatriate postings.

The expert informants also identified the increased frequency of the classic business trip – the frequent-flyer-type assignment – used by companies to build interpersonal relationships and for control purposes.

The reasons these expert informants attributed to increasing levels of international assignments, particularly the non-standard types, indicated that the extent to which international assignments are initiated by employers might also be changing. For instance, employees are more likely to initiate international transfer in some form or another now than they were three to five years ago. While this appears to contradict our earlier comments about the declining availability of staff willing to relocate internationally, the parameters for such self-initiated assignments are very much defined by the employees. As one Australian expert explained:

Employees are being a bit more selective about preserving their chosen lifestyle, rather than allowing the employer to dictate it.

It was apparent from the interview data the five Australian expert informants considered that virtual assignments are indeed a part of an international staffing repertoire.

A Danish Perspective

Based on the PricewaterhouseCoopers (2000) report, six of the Danish companies that had been part of the PricewaterhouseCoopers 2000 survey agreed to take part in an in-depth study to examine more fully the dynamics of expatriation. This study, conducted by the second author during 2001, involved two stages. Firstly, semi-structured, in-depth interviews were conducted with 11 HR directors of the six companies, except one where the interviewee was the person within the company in charge of expatriation management. From these interviews, it emerged that non-standard international assignments tended to fall outside the jurisdiction of the HR department in the case companies. Consequently, interviews with this group concentrated on traditional expatriate management issues and concerns, such as staff availability for international assignments. In response to this somewhat surprising result, however, further discussions with the participating HR managers were conducted and these were illuminating. For example, when informed as to how one multinational used virtual assignments, two HR managers related that their companies used virtual assignments in situations where employees had regional responsibilities. In the original interviews, this arrangement was not mentioned – it was not thought about as a 'virtual assignment'.

Concurrent interviews were conducted with 15 line managers across the six case companies about their attitude towards non-standard international assignments. In contrast to their HR counterparts, the line managers were more familiar with their employees' various experiences with non-standard assignments as they were more actively involved in selecting and deploying staff for non-standard international assignments. Thus, line managers could volunteer specific cases: for example, the use of commuter assignments (one case was an employee who worked three days in another Nordic country and two days in the Danish headquarters); and short-term international assignments.

The second part of the Danish study included a questionnaire sent to potential expatriates chosen by each case company's HR-division after consultation with relevant line managers. The main interest here was to gauge staff willingness to relocate internationally, and what types of assignment postings these potential international assignees were willing to accept. Of the 141 potential candidates surveyed, 70 percent answered that they would accept a virtual assignment, making it the most popular of the non-standard international assignments. 60 percent of the respondents would accept a short-term assignment, 41 percent a commuter assignment and 46 percent a rotational assignment. Further, while only four percent (five respondents) were prepared to state that they would *not* accept a long-term international assignment in the foreseeable future, the nature of the assignment seemed an important factor in determining staff availability.

In sum, by providing perspectives from HR and line managers and potential expatriates, the Australian and Danish studies confirmed the general trends exposed by broader surveys such as that conducted by PricewaterhouseCoopers. First, in interviews, Danish HR and line managers, and Australian expert informants, agreed that it has become more difficult to send people on foreign assignments. Second, prospective expatriates selected the virtual assignment as the most attractive option among the non-standard international assignments. This result strengthens the impression from interview data in the six Danish case companies that it is becoming more difficult to persuade young people to accept a traditional expatriate assignment. It also confirms the findings of the Pricewaterhouse Coopers surveys that virtual assignments were being considered by more companies as a solution to staff immobility.

Based on the data gained, a pilot study was conducted in early 2002 to explore issues surrounding the use of virtual assignments. This involved two interviews with Danish subsidiary staff of a large IT multinational. The firm was selected because was well known for using virtual assignments for project management and as a way of managing its regional offices. One interviewee managed the operations in the other three Nordic countries. It was therefore considered an appropriate pilot case site. Each interview took one-and-a-half hours. In the next section, data from these pilot interviews, combined with the findings of the broader studies referred to above, are used to support our exploration into the nature of the virtual assignment. For ease of reading, *italics* font is used when qualitative data, in the form of verbatim quotations from interviewees/respondents, is presented. To protect confidentiality, interviewees are identified by a country code – that is, D1 refers to Danish interviewee 1, A1 refers to Australian interviewee 1 – and company names are disguised.

Managing Virtually

By definition, the virtual assignee straddles both HQ/unit and foreign unit in a special way. For a majority of the time, the Virtual Assignee is physically located in the home unit, that may or may not be company headquarters – it could be in another subsidiary unit. In reality, the split between the country of living and the countries where the employee hold responsibilities is not that clear cut, because many people on virtual assignments also have some responsibilities in the country where they live.

It is important here to state that we are not assuming that all virtual assignments involve work in virtual teams. Even though it appears the terms are used interchangeably in the literature (see for example, Cascio 2000, Townsend/DeMarie/Hendrickson 1998), we make a distinction between virtual teams and Virtual Workgroups. Virtual team members remain in their geographically and organisationally distant locations but work on a defined project using telecommunications and information technologies – dispersed in terms of space in geographical isolation from each other, and operate asynchronously in terms of time (Montoya-Weiss/Massey/Song 2001). In the virtual assignment, only one member (the Virtual Assignee) is geographically distant. Virtual teams often remain together for the life of the project, whereas in the virtual assignment context, the work group is real – less transient in form and substance. It functions in the traditional co-located sense, a "powerful unit of collective performance" (Katzenbach/Smith 1993, p. 10), but not necessarily bound by the levels of commitment and synergistic performance terms associated with teams. While teams might feature within the Virtual Workgroup, we suggest that the relationship between the Virtual Assignee and the Virtual Workgroup does not *necessarily* equate to virtual teamwork.

The somewhat unique work arrangement that results from a virtual assignment poses both advantages and disadvantages for the Virtual Assignee, and the work groups involved in both the home and host locations. These are now discussed, with reference to Figure 1.

Figure 1. Factors Influencing Virtual Workgroup Relations

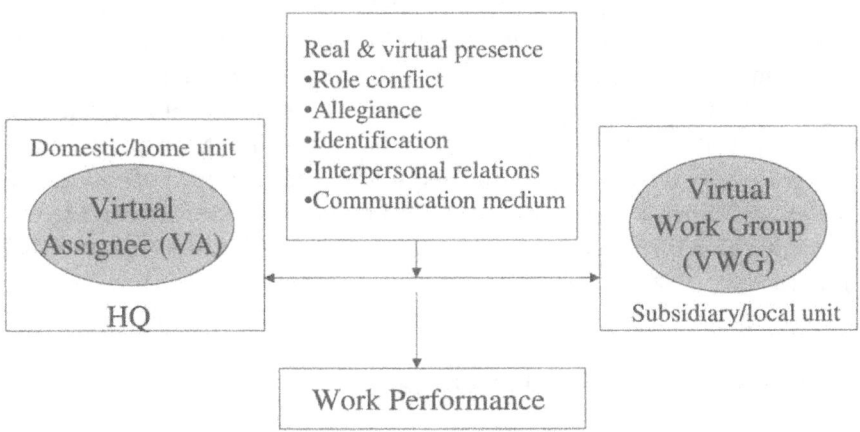

Real and Virtual Presence

The appeal of the virtual assignment, from the organisation's perspective, is that it either removes or lessens some of the barriers to the traditional assignment, particularly staff immobility and cost containment, due to savings on relocation expenses and other aspects of a traditional assignment, and accommodation of dual career concerns and other family-related barriers to staff mobility. At the same time, the organization can expect to reap at least some of the benefits usually accrued to the traditional expatriate assignment. For example, expatriates are at the boundary of the parent company and the local unit as they seek simultaneously to achieve headquarters goals while building and maintaining good relations with various stakeholders in the host location. This boundary-spanning role assists in transferring information and knowledge about the subsidiary environment to the centre, enhancing global control (Janssens 1994).

For the individual, there are many advantages to agreeing to manage virtually. The main attraction is not having to relocate to a foreign country, with the accompanying issues such as disruption to spouse/partner's career and childrens' education. In addition, the loss of visibility, often mentioned as a traditional expatriate concern as being 'out-of-sight, out-of-mind' would be lessened, as a Virtual Assignee is still visible in the home location. The dangers inherent in a lengthy period abroad, such as being passed over for promotion, and the nature of the repatriation position, are thereby lessened or negated. A similar argument could be mounted for other non-standard assignments, by nature of the shorter duration of the foreign assignment component.

Somewhat paradoxically, from a HQ perspective, one of the concerns of using expatriates on long-term assignments is that they may so identify with the foreign operation that they lose sight of headquarters' objectives, and the global perspective inherent in the expatriate role. This so-called 'going native' phenomenon is often cited as a reason for limiting the duration of the traditional expatriate assignments from three to five years (Black/Gregersen/Mendenhall 1992, Welch/Welch 1994). By remaining physically located in the home unit at least for the majority of the time, one would expect that the closer monitoring of the individual due to proximity would alert co-located workers to any signs of 'going native'. However, as Figure 1 shows, the real and virtual presence raises questions about loyalty which, in turn, may exacerbate critical aspects such as role conflict and dual allegiance.

Role Conflict, Dual Allegiance and Identification

The question of loyalty between home and host work units may contribute to intra-personal role conflict. Gregersen and Black (1990) discuss how an expatriate's role conflict can be engendered by dual allegiances to the home and host unit, with the potential of causing the expatriate to be pulled in two directions. These authors argue that having to 'choose sides' in conflict situations between headquarters and the subsidiary may provoke intra-personal role conflict, as the expatriate may be expected to show loyalty to headquarters' position. The Virtual Assignee may even be pulled in three directions – having to cater for global concerns (represented by headquarters), home work unit concerns and the concerns of the Virtual Workgroup – thus increasing the potential of intra-personal role conflict. This may be further exacerbated if, by identifying with the home unit or headquarters, the Virtual Assignee is perceived by the Virtual Workgroup concerned as an agent for headquarters rather than the work group's champion at headquarters. In the PricewaterhouseCoopers 2000 survey, 55% of responding firms that used virtual assignments reported that lack of assignee (Virtual Assignee) integration into the local workplace was a major problem. 35% of responding firms also mentioned resentment from host company employees as a further problem encountered in the use of Virtual Assignees.

Work time remains a finite resource despite recent technological developments and the placement of priorities may present often-conflicting loyalties and choices. The two Danish interviewees stressed the need to distribute one's time between work locations, and to cater for task and non-task performance when in the foreign location. For example:

> *Sometimes when I come to Stockholm I have to go out and have a beer with my people in Sweden and then go home next day* (D1).

Further, intra-personal role conflict may be heightened by a virtual assignment rather than lessened, simply because that is where the Virtual Assignee's primary responsibility and performance accountability lies. Vested self-interest may dictate placing primary allegiance with the Virtual Workgroup in the short-term, but generally one's career path is with the home unit, and ultimately with headquarters. A contributing factor to the Virtual Assignee's dilemma is that the virtual assignment requires frequent support visits to the foreign location, during which time the Virtual Assignee may foster an identify with the work unit, similar to that of a 'real' expatriate assignment. For the Virtual Assignee, identifying more with Virtual Workgroup members might well result in developing or increasing psychic, or mental, distance with those in the home office, even if it simultaneously reduces the psychic distance between the Virtual Assignee and the Virtual Workgroup. Where to place one's priorities and loyalties becomes as valid a concern as with traditional expatriate assignments.

The proportion of daily activities that is allocated to the Virtual Assignee's international responsibilities is another aspect to be considered. Conceivably, the greater the Virtual Assignee's international responsibilities, the more work time is spent interacting with the Virtual Workgroup, the less time there is available for interacting with co-located co-workers. Further, Virtual Workgroup members will expect the Virtual Assignee to champion their cause where necessary at the headquarters or home location. This may have important consequences for group dynamics and work performance, as a mutual lack of trust between group members might result (Jones/George 1998). Another danger is that Virtual Assignees may be treated as outliers – not accepted as full members of either the home unit or the host unit, by virtue not being one hundred percent present in either location, where time present physically is equated with the degree of organisational or unit commitment. In other words, at best the Virtual Assignee is regarded as a part-time worker in both locations. As one interviewee explained: *"You have to sell your self all the time in a virtual group"* (D2). It would seem that, to be effective, a virtual assignment would require deliberate investment in forums for face-to-face interaction and trust-building, particularly in the initial stages, to overcome some of the difficulties involved in a long distance working relationship.

From the perspective of the Virtual Workgroup, the real or virtual presence of the Virtual Assignee could be of relevance in determining identification to global operations. Reade's (2001a, b) work on the antecedents of identification in multinational corporations (MNCs) highlights the importance of fostering employee identification with the global level of the MNC in order to preserve overall cohesion. Her findings suggest "negative interpersonal relations with colleagues in the global network have a statistically significant negative impact on global identification" (2001b, p.1284). If this is indeed the case, then perceived negative relations with a Virtual Assignee located geographically distance will affect Virtual Workgroup members' identification with the global organization. Building the right work relationship between the Virtual Assignee and the Virtual Workgroup becomes a strategic issue. As Reade (2001a, p. 419) argues, strong local and global identification "may be an important ingredient not only for the success of the subsidiary but ultimately for the MNC as a whole".

Interpersonal Relations

Workgroup dynamics, social cohesion and positive interpersonal relations are well-recognised contributory factors to group performance. Despite members' separation, it is still possible to form group identity, as one Danish interviewee remarked:

> *A strong coherence can develop in a virtual group. It depends on the group. A good chemistry within a group is extremely important for the group's performance* (D2).

By its very nature though, the virtual assignment alters the processes by which a real group forms and operates. Firstly, geographical distance means that the normal daily interaction in the workplace that encourages social cohesion is diminished somewhat in the virtual context, as the following interviewee's comment reveals: "*One does not phone [a work colleague just] to ask how was the holiday*". The frequency and duration of supportive visits become an important group maintenance task, as the following interviewee explains:

> *When I travel, I don't get any "work" done. I mainly talk with people in my organisation. I don't go there only for the meetings. You have to know your people extremely well, otherwise you cannot deal with them* (D1).

Frequent visits are time consuming, as one of the Danish interviewees pointed out: *I have travelled 22 days in the first two months of this year* (D2). Naturally though, supportive visits to the host location provide the Virtual Assignee with more than the opportunity to forge social bonds. As Johannesen et al. (2001, p. 4) point out: "tacit knowledge is difficult to communicate to others as information, and can at best be difficult to digitalize". Such knowledge is highly person-bound. Face-to-face contact plays an important role in how information is exchanged, tacit knowledge is shared, and work is monitored (Roberts et al. 1998). In addition, the interview data suggests the necessity to build formal structures for operational and systemic procedures to support the lack of real presence of all group members when important decisions need to be made. For example:

> *If decisions are to be made during teleconferences, then all group members must know the* [underlying] *premises and know each other well* (D1).

Secondly, the virtual nature of the assignment may introduce or heighten areas for conflict. If the majority of a Virtual Assignee's time is spent in the home location, with daily interaction with Virtual Workgroup members largely work related, heavily reliant on the use of faxes, emails and telephone calls, the potential for misunderstanding and giving unintended offence increases. High-context cultures rely more heavily on one's ability to read the non-verbal cues than in low context cultures (Hall 1976). Such cues are missing from electronic media:

> *One cannot see their facial expression* [over the telephone] *although I think I am good at hearing voices* [picking up non-verbal cues]. *I can feel if there are problems* (D2).

Thirdly, being a Virtual Assignee requires more flexibility than in traditional assignments:

> *As a person you have to be incredibly flexible. If something goes wrong I must be able to take the plane to* [European city] *and phone my wife that I will not come back until 2–3 days later. When I was working* [as a traditional expatriate] *my work day was more structured* (D1).

Communication Medium

As Figure 1 illustrates, another factor that may influence the work relations between the Virtual Assignee and the Virtual Workgroup, is the communication medium used. In the virtual assignment situation, less direct communication channels become the important means of linking the two parties together so that the negative aspects of absence of daily physical presence is minimised. The PricewaterhouseCoopers survey data indicated that email, video conferencing and telephone calls are important media for communication between the Virtual Assignee and the Virtual Workgroup. This was borne out in our interview data. For example:

> *Communication is mainly conference calls and emails. Lots of decisions are made by conference calls* (D1).

Working virtually requires both the Virtual Assignee and the Virtual Workgroup to be comfortable with the various forms of electronic media, and may also place demands on work schedules and procedures. One interviewee stressed the time factor involved:

> *You have to be very much aware of how you use your time. I structure my time mainly according to topics. Monday we talk about opportunities. Tuesday about HR issues and so on. We know how long [a] time each phone meeting takes. Monday half an hour, Tuesday one hour. I spend a lot of time on the phone* (D1).

Using emails to communicate presented challenges for the Danish interviewees, as revealed by the following examples:

> *I can motivate people by emails* [by, for example,] *saying that they get so much money if the contract is signed, or I can follow up on things but I cannot make people run in the same direction by emails . . .*
> *Many [of my Virtual Workgroup] write all too many emails. It takes time to answer them.* (D1).

> *Emails . . . can easily give a wrong impression and convey a meaning that was not intended* (D2).

Interviewees also pointed out that the greater the physical distance between the Virtual Assignee and the Virtual Workgroup, the more use of emails, because of time differences. As one interviewee added: "*one does not call a colleague in the middle of the night, because it would influence his or her work the next day*". However, time differences can be utilized constructively – one can send an email at the end of the day so that a colleague can continue working on the matter on the other side of the globe. Of course, this assumes that emails will be answered, and there is a cultural element to be considered here. A Virtual Assignee interacting via email with Virtual Workgroup members in a situation that involves a large cultural distance may encounter difficulties[1].

Another medium of communication is via videoconferencing. 35% of responding firms in the PricewaterhouseCoopers 2000 survey indicated they encouraged the use of videoconferencing as a way of addressing the lack of face-to-face, daily contact inherent in the virtual assignment situation.

> *Virtual leadership can be done over long distances, but it is difficult. Last year I was involved with a customer who had a subsidiary both in the USA and Australia. In such a case one has to be extremely careful with the timing of teleconferences. It would not work over a long period of time.* (D2)

Videoconferencing is also used as a substitute for visits to a foreign location. As one Australian expert informant observed:

The advent [and] wider use of electronic communications ... [such as] videoconferencing means business [can be conducted] without hopping on an aeroplane to do it" (A1).

It is not, though, a perfect substitute for face-to-face communication and contact. As Kezsbom (2000, p. 34) points out, "even in the best of videoconferencing, facial expressions can be difficult to pick up if the transmission is poor, if someone is off camera, or when the mute button is pressed". Some people find videoconferences constraining and this may be reflected in their body language. Misunderstandings may arise if, for instance, discomfort with the medium is interpreted as discomfort with the person receiving the message. One Australian expert who had experience with this form of electronic communication, found that, along with its advantages, videoconferencing has:

[A] kind of mechanical aspect to it where you can see people but you feel like you're kind of game playing, almost role playing rather than engaging in real conversations. And you've got time limits set and you're subject to technology and that everything works properly (A2).

The Danish interviewees indicated a preference for using videoconferences to follow up earlier made decisions, but it was not considered as effective for the conduct of dialogues and discussions. Videoconferencing was useful for training purposes however. Frequent use of this medium, they both agreed, had allowed them to develop some competence in listening to the voices of their Virtual Workgroup members so that they had a 'feel' for attitudes and moods conveyed over the telephone.

Conclusions

The above exploration of the virtual assignment suggests that it may become an important component of the portfolio of non-standard options available to an internationalising firm. However, it is unlikely to completely replace the traditional expatriate assignment. There are several reasons for this conclusion. First, the limited available empirical evidence indicates an industry bias. For example, 69% of respondents in the PricewaterhouseCoopers 2000 survey who indicated using the virtual assignment were in the oil and gas industry. The Danish and Australian informants suggested that the IT industry lends itself to virtual management situations due, perhaps, to a general familiarity and ease with the communication techniques that support this work arrangement. For example, a Danish interviewee stated: *"More companies will come to work like us if they want to be international"*(D2).

Second, the nature of the task or work involved is another factor in determining its applicability: respondents in the PricewaterhouseCoopers survey indicated they were using virtual assignments to manage local operations (55%); for troubleshooting, establishing a global company culture, for project operations and to open new operations (35% for each of these respectively); 20% indicated they would use a virtual assignment to fill a skills gap, and 15% to train staff. Two of the Danish case companies indicated that some research and development activities lend themselves to the use of virtual teams and that the virtual assignment could be a viable extension of this work approach. Virtual assignments in the Danish IT company are used for leadership and coordination, such as managing regional offices.

Third, it is somewhat difficult at this stage to comment on managing virtual and traditional international assignments in foreign operations other than the wholly-owned context, as empirical work on staff transfers has been mainly confined to intra-MNC movements. Little work has been conducted into other modes – such as international joint ventures, international projects, international franchising, and the like – that require the use of international staff transfers (Welch/Welch 1994). Moreover, with the proliferation of non-traditional forms of multinational enterprise, such as strategic networks, the Virtual Assignee might not be so much a strategic reaction to cost containment and staff availability imperatives, but a fundamental strategic requirement to facilitate such flexible multinational forms. Some forms of foreign operation modes, such as project operations, may lend themselves to virtual assignments more than others. A virtual assignment may provide a low-risk way of assessing the feasibility of a new venture or mode of foreign operation, as the following comment from a respondent in the PricewaterhouseCoopers survey suggests: "When you're not sure how the project will go, virtual assignments can work [as a short term solution]". However, often the foreign client demands the physical presence of key project staff as a tangible signal of commitment to the project, thus reinforcing the use of traditional expatriate assignments.

Last, our Danish and Australian interviewees concurred that traditional international assignments will continue to be used for the global strategic purposes of filling staffing vacancies, employee development, and creating organisational networks, that can only be delivered through a real rather than a virtual presence. Traditional expatriate assignments provide actual international experience of working and managing in foreign environments, and facilitate the development of inter-unit networks, and informal communication and information flows that form a critical part of the MNC's control processes and mechanisms (Fenwick/De Cieri/Welch 1999), as indicated in the following interviewee comments:

> People who can reach high positions should be sent out on normal assignments... People come to know you... Networks are absolutely essential for how people manage themselves in [our company] (D2).

Traditional international assignments are important ... they promote your career opportunities ... During normal assignments you can build networks that you can use later. (D1).

In this day and age, to be successful in the corporation, you should have had your first international assignment by the age of about 35. It doesn't necessarily have to have been a three-year assignment but you should have lived offshore even if it's only for six months or so (A1).

Areas for Future Research

Given its newcomer status, and the relative lack of empirical work, it is not possible to make definitive, or normative, statements regarding how virtual assignments should be managed. Rather than offer somewhat speculative managerial implications, we make some suggestions for future research. Our albeit limited data indicate there may be important differences between a traditional expatriate and a virtual assignee, in terms of elements such as frequent traveling between home and host location, and the Virtual Assignee's non-permanent presence in the foreign location. A starting point for further research into the nature of the virtual assignment would be to further explore these differences through a comparative cohort study of traditional expatriates and virtual assignees. The expatriate management literature is replete with studies looking at expatriate selection criteria. In contrast, little is known about the skills and abilities that may be required to handle a virtual assignment, though there may be commonalities with the skills required to work in virtual teams. The two Danish interviewees stressed an ability to deal with people in a social as well as the work context, and to be able to build personal networks as essential skills for Virtual Assignees. Ease of using new communication technologies would seem to be another critical component. In addition, what training would be required to assist a Virtual Assignee and the Virtual Workgroup members achieve the desired level of performance? Such studies would need to include members of the Virtual Workgroup involved, and include cases where the Virtual Assignee has come from a subsidiary unit, rather than from headquarters. This approach would reflect that reality of international staff transfers – it is "three-way" traffic, not just unidirectional (HQ to subsidiary), but from subsidiary to HQ, and between subsidiary units.

The interview data from the six Danish case companies suggest that some HR departments may be isolated from the management of virtual and other non-standard international assignments, and that the deployment and management of employees on these non-standard assignments fall into the ambit of line managers. If this is indeed the situation, then future empirical studies should begin with relevant line managers. HR directors could be involved as part of data triangulation, depending on the level of the involvement of the HR department, its relative strategic position and profile within the company, and the level of non-standard assignment positions involved. The Danish IT company is a case in point as virtual assignments were common throughout the company and were used frequently for higher level positions such as that of regional manager.

In their 1994 article, Welch and Welch point to the seeming preoccupation of the general IHRM literature with traditional expatriate management issues at the expense of other forms of international assignments. It has been evident from our examination of the literature for the purpose of this article that this preoccupation persists. Little work has been done into the management and HRM issues pertaining to non-standard international assignments. This is perhaps a curious anomaly given that the PricewaterhouseCoopers surveys and the Australian and Danish studies point to the increased usage of these types of international assignments. There may be commonalities across these non-standard types – such as between commuters, frequent business travelers and virtual assignees – that would assist in their effective management. Future research that examined the nature of these assignment types in more depth – along the lines suggested for investigating the virtual assignment – would assist in our understanding of the commonalities and differences across all types of international assignments, and the management implications thereof.

In conclusion, the information and communication technology revolution, generating technologies such as desktop video conferencing, collaborative software, and internet/intranet facilities, has enabled internationalizing companies to experiment with alternative staffing arrangements. Virtual assignments indeed may be feasible, and in some instances, for some companies, a necessity of international life, but they are just one of many ways in which multinationals can staff foreign operations. Despite the drawbacks for the parties concerned, the traditional expatriate assignment has been a feature of international business for centuries. Harnessing 21st century technology may alter some of its nature and substance, but it is unlikely to make the traditional expatriate assignment redundant.

Endnote

1 Almost on a weekly basis, one the authors of this paper receives phone calls from Danish companies asking why Chinese entities do not answer their emails. Basically the Chinese prefer to meet and come to know people before they begin exchanging emails.

References

Black, J. S./Gregersen, H. B./Mendenhall, M. E. *Global Assignments: Successfully Expatriating and Repatriating International Managers*, San Francisco: Jossey-Bass 1992.

Cascio, W., Managing a Virtual Workplace, *Academy of Management Executive,* 14, 3, 2000, pp. 81–90.

Chen, M-J./Farh, J-L./MacMillan, I. C., An Exploration of the Expertness of Outside Informants, *Academy of Management Journal,* 36, 6, 1993, pp. 1614–1632.

Dowling P.J/Welch D. E., Schuler R. S., *International Human Resource Management: Managing People in a Multinational Context*, third edition, South-Western College 1998.

Edström, A./Galbraith, J. R., Transfer of Managers as a Coordination and Control Strategy in Multinational Organizations, *Administrative Science Quarterly,* 22, 2, 1977, pp. 248–263.

Fenwick, M./De Cieri, H., Welch, D., Cultural and Bureaucratic Control in MNEs: The Role of Expatriate Performance Management, *Management International Review,* 39, 1999, pp.107–124.

Gregerson, H./Black, J. S., A Multifaceted Approach to Expatriate Retention in International Assignment, *Group and Organization Studies,* 15, 4, 1990, pp. 461–485.

Hall, E., *Beyond Culture*, New York: Doubleday 1976.

Harris, H., Women in International management. Why Are They Not Selected, in Brewster, C., Harris, H. (eds.), International HRM: Contemporary Issues in Europe, London: Routledge, 1999, pp. 259–276.

Janssens, M., Evaluating International Managers' Performance: Parent Company Standards as a Control Mechanism, *The International Journal of Human Resource Management,* 5, 4, 1994, pp. 853–873.

Johannessen, J. A./Olaisen, J./Olsen, B., Mismanagement of Tacit Knowledge: The Importance of Tacit Knowledge, the Danger of Information Technology, and What to Do about It, *International Journal of Information Management*, 21, 2001, pp. 3–20.

Jones, G. R./George, J. M., The Experience and Evolution of Trust: Implications for Cooperation and Teamwork, *Academy of Management Review,* 23, 3, 1998, pp. 531–546.

Katzenbach, J. R./Smith, D. K., The Discipline of Teams, *Harvard Business Review,* 71, 2, 1993, pp. 111–120.

Kezsbom, D. S., Creating Teamwork in Virtual Teams, *Cost Engineering,* 42 10, 2000, pp 33–36.

Latta, G., Expatriate Policy and Practice: A Ten Year Comparison of Trends. *Compensation and Benefits Review,* 31, 4, 1999, pp. 35–39.

Miles, M.B./Huberman, M., *Qualitative Analysis*, second edition, Thousand Oaks, CA: Sage 1994.

Montoya-Weiss, M. M./Massey, A. P./Song, M., Getting It together: Temporal Coordination and Conflict Management in Global Virtual Teams, *Academy of Management Journal,* 44, 6 2001, pp.1251–1262.

Novicevic, M. M./Harvey, M.G., The Emergence of the Pluralism Construct and the Inpatriation Process, *International Journal of Human Resource Management,* 12, 3, 2001, pp. 333–356.

Ondrack, D., International Transfers of Managers in North American and European MNEs, *Journal of International Business Studies,* 16, 3, 1985, pp. 1–19.

Price Waterhouse, *International Assignments: European Policy and Practice,* Price Waterhouse Europe 1997.

PricewaterhouseCoopers, *Managing a Virtual World: International Non-standard Assignments, Policy and Practice*, PricewaterhouseCoopers Europe 2000.

Reade, C., Dual Identification in Multinational corporations: Local Managers and Their Psychological Attachment to the Subsidiary versus the Global Organization, *International Journal of Human Resource Management,* 12, 3, 2001a, pp. 405–425.

Reade, C. Antecedents of Organizational Identification in Multinational Corporations: Fostering Psychological Attachment to the Local Subsidiary and the Global Organization, *International Journal of Human Resource Management,* 12, 8, 2001b, pp. 1269–1291.

Roberts, K/Kossek, E. E./Ozeki, C., Managing the Global Workforce: Challenges and Strategies, *Academy of Management Executive* 12, 4, 1998, pp. 93–106.

Tung, R., American Expatriates Abroad: From Neophytes to Cosmopolitans, *Journal of World Business*, 33, 2, 1998, pp. 125–144.
Townsend, A./DeMarrie, S./Hendrickson, A., Virtual Teams: Technology and the Workplace of the Future, *Academy of Management Executive*, 12, 3, 1998, pp. 17–29.
Welch, D. E., HRM Implications of Globalization, *Journal of General Management*, 19, 4, 1994, pp. 52–67.
Welch, D. E./Welch, L. S., Linking Operation Mode Diversity and IHRM, *International Journal of Human Resource Management*, 5, 4, 1994, pp. 911–926.
Worm, V./Selmer, J./de Leon, C., Human Resource Development for Localization: European Multinational Corporations in China, in Kidd, J./Li, X./Richter, F. (eds.), *Advances in Human Resource Management in Asia*, London: Palgrave 2001, pp. 188–211.

Volker Mahnke/Markus Venzin

The Internationalization Process of Digital Information Good Providers

Abstract

- This study examines how product characteristics shape the internationalization process of digital information good providers.

- An exploratory case study of eBay's internationalization process serves to illustrate the need for, and possibilities of, theory development to extend and augment current research by integrating product characteristics.

Key Results

- It is shown how three streams of literature – stage models of internationalization, internalization theory, and international new venture research – all seeking to explain the pace and modalities of internationalization, relate to the internationalization of digital information good providers.

- The results indicate possibilities for new theory development based on product characteristics in general and digital good characteristics in particular.

Authors

Volker Mahnke, Associate Professor, Department of Informatics, Copenhagen Business School, Copenhagen – FDB, Denmark.
Markus Venzin, Assistant Professor, Department of Strategy & Entrepreneurship, Universita Luigi Bocconi, Milano, Italy.

Introduction

Research on international expansion starting in the 1970s has focused on explaining the slow and incremental internationalisation process of typically large manufacturing firms (Johanson/Wiedersheim 1975, Buckley/Casson 1976, Rugman 1981, Dunning 1988, Johanson/Vahlne 1990, Andersen 1993) followed by a period of empirical corroboration. Relying on organizational learning aspects and transaction cost theory, this literature addresses determinants of entry mode (in a single foreign market) and entry patterns (across foreign markets) such as uncertainty, control needs, resource commitment and, most importantly, largely tacit foreign market knowledge. Much of this literature has been developed in the context of large firms that provide physical goods. By contrast, this paper is concerned with the question of *how the characteristics of digital information goods influence the internationalization process of companies involved in their provision*.

Interestingly, from the late 1980's on, researchers have increasingly addressed small firms that operated internationally early in their existence despite limited resources and capabilities in industries including high-technology, software, art, and craft (Sharma/Johanson 1987, Welch/Luostarinen 1988, McDougall 1989, Oviatt/McDougall 1994, McDougall et al. 1994, Bell 1995, Knight/Cavusgil 1996, Coviello/Munro 1997, Madsen/Servais 1997, Coviello/McAuley 1999). Research on such international new ventures[1] observes accelerated internationalisation and to some extent a more frequent use of hybrid governance structures (e.g. Joint Ventures) during international expansion. Theoretical explanations offered for accelerated internationalization emphasize the increasing importance of network relations, industrial conditions, manager/entrepreneur's capabilities and mind set, and, perhaps, most importantly technological change (Oviatt/McDougall 1999, Knight/Cavusgil 1997). For example, several innovations that have improved the speed and lowered the cost of international communications would include the telegraph, the telephone, fax machines, and most recently the Internet.

The 'international new venture literature' has accumulated evidence that questions explanations and predictions of traditional literature on international expansion (see Coviello/McAuley 1999). It also identifies factors that are instrumental in developing a more context sensitive and comprehensive theory of the internationally expanding firm. Unfortunately, this literature does not address the product characteristics of digital information goods and their impact on the internationalization process of the expanding firm. In particular, Oviatt and McDougall (1999) have recently proposed that the several explanatory factors discussed above are increasing in importance relative to tacit market knowledge as suggested in traditional models of internationalization. Nonetheless, while „. . .firms that are committed to multinational markets from their inception may internationalize rapidly through a simultaneous combination of modes...we have little understanding about why combinations are chosen and which ones are typical and successful" (Oviatt/McDougall 1999, p. 6). Thus the key contributions of this literature may be seen in shedding new light on the pace rather than the modalities of internationalization.

In the mid 1990's, new firms began to commercialize technological opportunities associated with the Internet. Yahoo!, AOL, and eBay have several things in common. Software at their core, they make their money from the transactions or traffic that their software enables, they provide digital information goods in several forms, they are barely in business for a decade, and all three expanded rapidly in international markets. For example, founded in 1993, Yahoo! is present in 24 countries overseas. Founded in 1985 AOL became in little more than a decade the world leader in online services and serves the largest global online community. While these are admittedly diverse examples, they nonetheless exhibit a crucial similarity – they provide digital information goods on an international scale.

In this context, perhaps most significantly, technological change may be the foundation of a refined theory of internationalization (Oviatt/McDougall 1999). For example, new communication technologies such as the Internet allows small firms to become international via a website, and communication costs are reduced in international operations (Knight/Cavusgil 1997). Internet technology makes new forms of business possible such as the provision of digital information goods – the focal concern of this paper. For example, web technology allows auctions to be done in ways that are impossible in the physical world. However, as argued by Oviatt and McDougall (1999), changing technology, while serving as a foundation, cannot by itself explain accelerated internationalization (p.12). In this article, it is the internationalization process of companies seeking to exploit technological opportunities through new and innovative digital information goods on an international scale that constitute the context for theory development. By integrating digital good characteristics in a theory of international expansion, we respond to Madsen and Servais (1997) who critically remark that many studies in the new international venture literature are rather descriptive without a well-developed theoretical frame of reference. By implication, "...further studies should be more theory driven than the previous ones reported" (p. 580).

Building on the work of Varian and Shapiro (1999) and Bakos and Brynjolfsson (2000) on digital information goods, the current article suggests to establish a theoretical link between digital information good characteristics and the pace and entry modes of the internationally expanding firm. By stressing the relevance of product characteristics in general[2] and digital information good characteristics in particular, we use an exploratory case study[3] of eBay as an illustration and context for theory development.

We seek to highlight the key points of correspondence and discrepancy between eBay's internationalisation process and three literature-streams (internationalization theory, internalization theory, and research on international new ventures) to stress the importance of digital information goods for understanding the internationalization process of their provider. By assessing eBay's internationalization process against the three perspectives, the objective is to use the company as a specific context for theory development rather than to describe the company comprehensively. Thus, we will be selective, stressing empirical facts that are relevant to our theoretical argument, thereby presenting only a partial picture of the complex company.

To anticipate our argument, we will contrast eBay's internationalization process (i) with internationalization theory to explicate how digital information good characteristics shed light on the company's rapid pace of internationalization, (ii) with internalization theory to highlight how the company's choices of entry modes in alternative international markets are influenced by product characteristics, and (iii) with the 'new international venture' literature to offer a complementary explanation of rapid internationalization. The discussion shows that a more satisfying and contextual sensitive theory of international expansion benefits from the consideration of product characteristics to accommodate new and emergent forms of doing business on an international scale. The remainder of this article is structured as follows. First, we outline digital information good characteristics and their economic properties that may act as modifiers and possibly serve to extend current internationalization theory. Next, we contrast eBay's internationalization process with three streams of literature that seek to explain the pace and modalities of internationalization to show how they relate to the internationalization of digital information good providers. Finally, we identify and discuss key elements for a theory of internationalization of digital information good providers. Conclusions follow. this article is structured as follows. First, we outline digital information good characteristics and their economic properties that may act as modifiers and possibly serve to extend current internationalization theory. Next, we contrasts eBay's internationalization process to show how the three streams of literature that seek to explain the pace and modalities of internationalization relate to the internationalization of digital information good providers. Finally we identity and discuss key elements for a theory of internationalization of digital information good providers. Conclusions follow.

Digital Information Good Characteristics and Firms' Internationalization Process

For the purpose of this article, digital information goods – from web pages offering auctions through software, music, and movies – are broadly defined as expeience goods encoded as a string of bits (Varian/Shapiro 1999, Bakos/Brynjolfsson 2000).[4] Digital information goods differ from other goods in several dimension and their economic implication, including their experience good character, transportation costs, (re-) production-, and product adaptation costs (see Shapiro/Varian 1999, Bakos/Brynjolfsson 2000).

Experience Good Character

Digital information goods are often experience goods, which are signified by difficulties of consumers to evaluate such goods by sight, taste or touch before consumption (Nelson 1970). Who after all can assess the (dis-) pleasure of watching 'American Beauty' or 'Jurassic Park' lest one sees the movies? Likewise, trading through eBay auctions is a unique experience, the value judgment of which may depend on consumer expectation regarding speed, payment security, number and quality of offers etc. The more frequent one trades, the more predictable the quality of the auction experience becomes, but, nonetheless there remains uncertainty as every new auction is a new experience.

Digital information goods often require sellers to induce buyers to acquire information before consumption to facilitate the first experience. Various strategies to do so involve sharing information content (e.g. free samples of software, free tunes of a new CD via radio, a web page for the latest movie, free listing of seller items on auction sites). Such marketing efforts are usually cheap because of low marginal costs and effective in circumventing the experience good problem. Alternatively, branding and advertising are more expensive possibilities, but both signal quality to customers. By implication, in the presence of information costs, consumers may find it useful to rely on a firm's reputation while firms seek to induce customers through branding and advertising. Because digital information goods are also associated with complementary learning investments by consumers, for example in brand recognition, there are substantial economies of scope in advertising and branding of digital information goods. If building brands is expensive, international brand leverage is a formidable way to reap economies of scope.

Moreover, while the internationalization process of a firm may depend on the costs and possibilities of acquiring market knowledge (Johanson/Vahlne 1990), the cost and possibilities of customer learning about the firm's products may be equally important. Once customers have learned how to use a digital information good, an auction site or software for example, they are hesitant to switch to another one because of the hassle of new learning. For example, to post a single antique toaster, eBay asks a minimum of 50 questions at the start. In addition, and perhaps even more important, are the switching costs that relate to transaction records and trader reputation in the case of online auctions. When switching costs lead to lock-in effects, firms have to offer a huge advantage and/or compensate for switching costs to attract consumers from competitors. Moreover, because attention is a limiting factor when there is abundant information (Davenport/Beck 2001), rapid spread of digital information goods may require advertising and fast market penetration to pre-empt attention space of customers. In sum, the presence of information costs, customer lock-in, and economies of scope in branding may influence the pace of international expansion and entry modes chosen. Thus we suggest with regards to the internationalization process of digital good providers:

P1: Digital information good providers seek to enter foreign markets through entry modes that allow (a) control for branding and advertising strategies, and (b) gaining access to locked-in customer bases.

Transportation Costs

The digital nature of online-services allows for higher speed and lower costs of transportation compared to physical goods. For example, unlike agricultural goods, digital information goods do not perish or loose value during transport. Unlike the transport of heavy physical goods, mistakes in delivery (e.g. timing, dislocation) of digital information goods can be easily corrected and traced. In addition, issues of storing, inventory management and logistics are of little concern to digital information good providers. While transportation costs matter for digital information good providers, they matter far less compared to physical good providers. Where transportation costs are low, the need to locate facilities in proximity to particular markets, or the need to be very selective with choices of in-market locations may be a lesser concern. For example, whereas personal contact and local proximity between the producer and consumer appear to be an important aspect for many physical good providers and services (Buckley et al. 1992), it does not seem to play a decisive role in the provision of digital information goods. By implication, psychic distance (Johanson/Vahlne 1990) may matter less because decisions on location, storing and distribution are less important to digital good providers.

Transportation costs of digital information goods are not zero, however. Instead, they depend on the type of information technology (hardware and software) as well as the telecommunication network the client and service provider are using for data transfer. For some online services, a regular analogue voice telephony with a transmission capacity of 56 kbps may already satisfy the needs of most clients. To increase the speed of transfer, clients may choose to get connected with ISDN technology (56–128 kbps), ADSL (1.5–8 Mbps downstream and 12–500 kbps upstream), cable modems (1.2–27 Mbps downstream and 128–10 Mbps upstream), or, with the extreme satellite (400 kbps downstream and 56 kbps upstream via analogue voice telephony). Further increases in transmission speed can be expected from technological advance (e.g. UMTS). For example, streamed videos illustrating products offered in online auctions are too slow in transmission and have a too low quality via telephone connections. By implication, the kind of online services that can be offered to particular clients depends on transmission capacity, speed, and costs that are largely determined by competition among complementary services providers (e.g. Dixit/Nalebuff 1991). In addition, constraints in available infrastructure effectively limit market size for digital information good providers. Thus we suggest with regards to the internationalization process of digital information good providers:

P 2: Digital information good providers select foreign markets for entry that have high Internet penetration and advanced telecommunication infrastructure.

(Re-) production Costs and Competitive Dynamics

Digital information goods are often costly to produce but cheap to reproduce (Arrow 1997).[5] A movie costs hundreds of million US dollars to produce, but only little to copy on video and even less when distributed through streaming technology over the Internet. Likewise, software, news, and auction sites exhibit relatively high fix costs much of which are sunk and low marginal cost of re-production. To be sure, digital information good providers have to make capacity investments in hardware and software that also depend on the traffic volumes on websites. But marginal costs of serving additional users and the traffic they cause are low compared to required up front investments. High fixed costs and negligible marginal costs provide a vast potential for economies of scale in production of digital information goods. Physical goods by contrast usually exhibit "diminishing returns to scale", because from a certain point up, unit costs tend to rise. Thus, the cost structure of digital information good providers may also provide a powerful incentive to penetrate markets rapidly for reasons of minimum efficient scale.

Not only are digital information goods subject to supply side economies of scale, they often also exhibit demand side economies of scale or network effects – "the utility that a user derives from consumption of a good increases with the number of other agents consuming the good." (Katz/Shapiro 1985, p. 424). For example, the benefit of any particular user of eBay's online auction increases with the number of other users. Likewise, the value of software packages increases as more people use them. While other than digital information good providers may also enjoy network effects in businesses such as gas, electricity, or telecommunication, they are more prevalent in digital information goods because of their cost structure.

Combination of demand-side and supply-side economies of scale can lead to very powerful market positions of digital information good providers. This is because higher sales reduce total production costs per unit and at the same time also make the product even more valuable to current and new users. If this is the case, there is substantial potential for first mover advantages that may lead, in the extreme, to temporary monopolies in particular markets (Lieberman/Montgomery 1998, Liebowitz/Margolis 1995). Network effects, customer lock-in, and scale effects in productions can act as entry barriers to lock out late moving competitors from particular markets.

Competitive dynamics work with accelerated speed in product market for digital information goods because imitation barriers (Rumelt/Lippman 1982) are low. To the extent that digital information goods are easy to re-produce, they may be also easy to copy by competitors if they rest on common knowledge. Estimates of damages due to illegal copying of software amounted to US $ 11 billion in 1998. To replicate music stored in string of bits takes little more than a piece of software (e.g. witness recent law suits between Napster and the music industry), while imitating a complex physical good often takes years of effort. Likewise, to imitate an auction format is relatively easy compared to replicating complex machinery. By implications, sustainable competitive advantage is unlikely to stem from particular product features (e.g. particular auction formats that may be easy to copy) or from general IT skills in programming that are widely available. This, in turn, stresses the relative importance of other sources of competitive advantage such as branding, management of the client base, and network effects in markets for digital information goods. Thus we suggest with regards to the internationalization process of digital information good providers:

P3: Digital information good providers seek to penetrate foreign markets rapidly and through entry modes that allow them to benefit from economies of scale in production and demand (network effects), as well as industrial networks.

Product Adaptation Costs and Versioning

Because marginal costs of re-producing information goods are low, cost-based pricing schemes find their limits. For digital information good providers, however, product versioning and product adaptations can be cheaper and faster achieved. This opens up new pricing and marketing possibilities based on perceived customer value. Possibilities, as Bakos and Brynjolfsson (1999) suggest, include time based versioning (e.g. movie producers sell movies at a higher price to cineastes and latter for a lower price to less interested consumers), dis-aggregation of previously packaged information content (such as separating specialized news from previously aggregated news papers or journal articles), bundling of information according to consumers interest (e.g. information services like Reuters and Forester offer tailor made information packages that are sold to different industry segments), as well as rapid product adaptation according to instant consumer feedback (e.g. adapting or adding an auction category to a web site is far easier relative to changing a product design of specialized machinery).

Data on customers can also be exploited far more readily by digital information good providers for product adaptation in addition to the possibility of selling such data. For example, eBay charges final value fees for each successful transaction, has customer feedback forums, and monitors online transactions. These can be used for real-time learning about customer preferences and product adaptation because transactions can be easily tracked at low costs (e.g. through collaborative filtering technologies). Low cost of learning for product adaptation is facilitated not just by monitoring transaction quantities, but also through monitoring web pages customers visit, how much time they spend there and what fields they click on. This can produce customer data that is almost instantly available and allow rapid change of product specifications and features. By contrast, providers of physical goods usually utilize more expensive and slower methods such as surveys, interviews, sales force reports to gather customer feedback. By implication, when gathering customer feedback is cheap, and product features are easy to adapt, digital information good providers face lower costs of experimenting with product designs and real time learning for product adaptation compared to physical good providers. Thus we suggest with regards to the internationalization process of digital information good providers:

P4: Digital information good providers enter foreign markets more rapidly than physical good providers because of the possibility of low learning costs and rapid post-entry product adaptations.

eBay's Internationalization Process in Three Perspectives

To explain the importance of product characteristics in general and digital information good characteristics with particular reference to the internationalization process of the expanding firm, the following section highlights key points of correspondence and discrepancy between eBay's internationalization process and three literature-streams: internationalization theory, internalization theory, and research on international new ventures. Focus is on to international expansion patterns (across countries) and entry mode choices (in single foreign markets). Our product-characteristics based explanations may appear as a difference of degree rather than in kind relative to existing literature. Nonetheless, we hope to show that a theory of international expansion benefits from the consideration of product characteristics to accommodate new and emergent forms of doing business on an international scale.

Volker Mahnke/Markus Venzin

The Internationalization Process of eBay

eBay is a digital information good provider and pioneered online person-to-person trading by developing a web based community in which buyers and sellers are brought together in an efficient and entertaining web based auction format in a way not possible before Internet technology. Its web-based auction-style shopping platform facilitates a marketplace for products ranging from collectible items, such as antiques, coins and memorabilia, to automobiles and fine art. Sellers from around the world – individuals as well as small businesses – have used the auctions to enter vast markets far beyond their local reach. For example, a rare record dealer in Omaha using a web auction can sell his hard-to-find Frank Sinatra LPs from bidders in Paris or Moscow or Hong Kong, or a Belgian camera dealer can auction his antique lenses to a photography buff in London or Atlanta or Manila. Nonetheless, the main share of trade is conducted within countries (90%) rather than across the countries (10%) in which eBay has established as presence.

In essence, however, eBay is no more than software on a web server accompanied by a strong brand. Leaving inventory carrying costs, distribution risks, vendor management issues to those who participate in auctions, it has created a web based business model that shows that the web can create efficient markets where none existed before. Sellers pay the company for the privilege of setting up their own auctions, buyers use eBay's software to place bids. When the auction is over, the seller and the winning bidder negotiate payment and shipping between them, eBay never touches the goods. For this matchmaking service, eBay takes between 7% and 8% of the sale price. In addition, the company begins charging listing fees 9–12 month after launching a site in a particular location or a new category. Most of the value that eBay realizes from its transactions is in the final value fee. While the amount may be small, incremental revenues without corresponding incremental costs fall straight to the bottom line. High yields accompanied by stock issues in 1998 and 1999, provided substantial financial pockets for rapid international expansion. Founded in 1995, eBay in addition to the U.S. marketplace has expanded its platform internationally, operating country sites in fifteen international markets including Germany, France, Taiwan, Austria, Switzerland, UK, Italy, Australia, Korea, and New Zealand.

Internationalization of eBay has been initiated in late 1998, partly motivated by increasing competition by Amazon, Yahoo!, FairMarket, AuctionWatch, and Microsoft in the still growing home market. International expansion has since then evolved rapidly through growing user communities from the ground up, acquisition of local organizations, and partnership with local companies. Today eBay operates the world's leading trading community and marketplace on the Internet. In addition to eBay's US marketplace, which includes specialized local and regional communities, eBay has expanded its platform internationally, operating country sites in fifteen international markets including Germany, France, Austria, Switzerland, UK, Italy, Australia, Korea, Taiwan, and New Zealand.

In late 1998, eBay's efforts to expand internationally into Canada and the United Kingdom relied on building new user communities. The first step in establishing these communities was creating customized pages for users in those countries. These home pages were designed to provide content and categories locally customized to the needs of users in specific countries, while providing them with access to a global trading community based on eBay's infrastructure systems. Local customization in the United Kingdom was facilitated through the use of local management, grassroots and online marketing, and participation in local events. In February 1999, eBay partnered with PBL Online, a leading Internet company in Australia, to offer a customized Australian and New Zealand eBay home page. When the site went live in October 1999, transactions were denominated in Australian dollars and, while buyers could bid on auctions anywhere in the world, they could also search for items located exclusively in Australia. Further, local chat boards were designed to facilitate interaction between Australian users, and country-specific categories, such as Australian coins and stamps as well as cricket and rugby memorabilia, were offered. In June 1999 eBay acquired Germany's largest online person-to-person trading site, alando.de AG for US $ 50 million in stocks that had good traffic, but little revenue. eBay's management handled the transition of service in a manner calculated to be smooth and painless for alando.de AG's users while users would have to comply with eBay rules and regulations. The only significant change for alando.de AG's 50,000 registered users, was that of being automatically transferred to eBay's URL to transact their business. Only a year after crossing the Atlantic, eBay conquered Germany and erased the lead of Britain's QXL.com PLC, a British competitor. It started heading into France to take on iBazar, France's top auction site during spring 2001.

Although eBay opened a French site in 2000, capturing substantial market share in France as Europe's third largest online commerce markets has been impeded as iBazar – a leading provider of online trading services in Europe and Brazil – had anticipated eBay's arrival and acquired the domain name eBay.fr in 1998. The battle for supremacy in Europe's on-line auction market may have been decided in spring 2001 when eBay agreed to pay US $ 112 million in stock for iBazar bringing together two established web auction sites under a single strong brand in Europe. For the time being, iBazar is not expected to contribute to profits in the short term as most of its local sites will continue to work separately, while eBay works on system integration and implementing listing fees. Similar to eBay's acquisition of alando.de, the national brand will be maintained in the short term to leverage local brand recognition before eventually converting it to the eBay name. Through iBazar's acquisition, eBay has gained market leadership in Belgium, Brazil, Netherlands, Portugal, Spain, France, Italy, and Sweden, adding further to eBay's market leadership position in Australia, Canada, Germany, Korea and the UK.

Doing business in Europe has been complicated, however. In the US, four million auction participants each day can pay online through credit card or electronic check as a direct debit. For merchants, credit cards are expensive, but with direct debit, where a buyer authorizes a payment directly from a checking account, costs are small. The alternative is mailing a money order. With its one-third ownership of Billpoint, Wells Fargo is the bank that clears the eBay buyer's electronic check requests through what is called the Automated Clearing House (ACH), the network shared by thousands of US banks and the US government. There is no shared European ACH-style network, despite attempts by the European Union (EU) to encourage the banks across Europe to uniformly connect their proprietary networks to share direct debit information. When banks do manage to process these electronic check requests – which can be an uncertain and lengthy process – it can cost the customer a US $ 30 service fee, discouraging trade. Another roadblock, are the differing regulations in European nations, despite the existence of the EU and the Euro. For instance, regulatory authorities in Germany historically haven't allowed an online merchant to accept direct debit authorizations without the account holder signing a paper document – something not required in the US. However, Europe is saddled with at least 27 differing direct-debit networks, plus legal rules for ACH that differ from country to country.

To establish an Asian presence, in February 2000 eBay formed a joint venture with NEC to launch eBay Japan. According to the new CEO of eBay Japan, Merle Okawara, NEC was pleased to help eBay in leveraging the tried-and-trusted eBay business model to provide Japanese consumers with access to a global community of active online buyers and sellers. In customizing the site to the needs of Japanese users, eBay wrote the content exclusively in Japanese and allowed users to bid in yen. The site had over 800 categories ranging from internationally popular categories (such as computers, electronics, and Asian antiques) to categories with a local flavour (such as Hello Kitty, Pokemon and pottery). The eBay Japan site also debuted a new merchant-to-person concept known as "super shops", which allowed consumers to bid on items listed by companies. After two years of trying to gain market share from Yahoo! Japan, the online auction leader in Japan, eBay decided to close its operations in the region during spring 2002. This was somewhat of a disappointment as Japan represents the world's second largest eCommerce market, but management has spent a significant amount of time, effort and money in this region without gaining any competitive stronghold against Yahoo!. The difficulties in Japan exemplify the challenges of operating internationally, as well as the high barriers to entry in the online auction market that result from the network effect, i.e., buyers go where sellers are and vice versa. The company conceded that it also stumbled in executing its strategy in the market by not sufficiently adapting the eBay Japan site for the Japanese market and lacking network economies.

In early 2001, by taking advantage of low share prices of Asian clones, eBay entered Korea, through establishing a majority stakeholder position in Internet Auctions, Ltd., Korea's leading online auction site. Internet Auction Co. is Korea's largest auction company, with about 2.8 million users and an average of 450,000 listings. Prior to the acquisition both Internet Auction and eBay had announced aspirations to become the dominant player in Asia markets including Korea, Japan, Taiwan, Hong Kong and China. Without consolidation both companies would have competed head on. Shareholders of Internet Auction welcomed eBay's substantial financial means, strong brand name, and substantial knowledge and experience in running web based auctions that are expected to contribute to circumvent Internet Auctions system outages that were due to computer glitches. eBay on the other hand sees the Korean market as bridgehead to further Asian expansion and is keen to benefit from the advanced escrow system deployed by Internet Auction as well as its strong foothold in Japan where Internet Auction has developed relationships with Hitachi and Marubeni.

As it is working through the hard lessons it learned in the Japanese market, eBay Inc. is putting its effort into new ventures in the Asian market. During early 2002 eBay announced it agreed to acquire NeoCom Technology Co., Ltd., for US $ 9.5 million in cash to enter the Taiwanese market which represents the third largest and fastest growing eCommerce market in Asia. NeoCom is a Taiwanese operator of the auction Web sites uBid.com.tw and Bid.com.tw, Taiwan's first two person-to-person trading platforms were already launched in October 1998. eBay also bought a 33% interest in EachNet.com, the leading online auction site in China. The moves further increase eBay's presence in the Asia-Pacific area.

eBay has been aggressive in expanding in overseas markets using simultaneous entry in several international markets. The recent additions of Korea, Italy, France, Austria, Taiwan, and China give eBay a dominant presence in eight of the top ten international markets outside of the US. New user growth in Europe is 50% faster than the rest of eBay, while gross merchandise sales are growing 135% faster. More importantly, however, the company is beginning to monetize international growth by gradually introducing standardized listing fees on all its international sites and by further connecting its scalability IT infrastructure and systems to acquired operations abroad. Nonetheless, eBay faces a significant amount of competition, especially as it expands overseas, where local competitors have first mover advantages and strong local brands. In many countries, eBay will have to compete with local companies who understand the local market better. Thus, after a period of fast international expansion (1999–2002) there are rising concerns whether continued expansion can be profitably managed. eBay is already spending much of its sales and advertising budget overseas. Clearly, eBay cannot hope to attract new customers and build a brand in foreign markets as cheaply as the Internet hype allowed in the US where brand building proceeded at low costs. There are also concerns with regards to eBay's international 'growth-through-acquisition strategy' as this eliminates local competitors to leave the company in many markets alone to build out the online auction category on a country-by-country basis. Nonetheless, it also allowed eBay despite lacking first mover advantage to become the leading online auction site in Europe and Asia.

eBay in the Perspective of the Current Internationalization Theory

Albeit variously criticized[6] there is a fairly solid core of knowledge about international expansion represented by two established streams of literature. *Stage models of internationalization* (e.g. Johanson/Wiedersheim-Paul 1975, Johanson/Vahlne 1990) offer prediction about entry patterns (across foreign markets) and entry mode choices (in single markets) based on theories of organizational learning (Cyert/March 1963). The *internalization theory* of the MNC is concerned with entry mode choices in single markets based on transaction cost analysis (e.g. Williamson 1975, Hymer 1966, Buckley/Casson 1976, Rugman 1981, Dunning 1988). In both theories lacking foreign market knowledge is a central construct. Lacking foreign market knowledge increases risk exposure to the internationally expanding firms, to which it responds through either limited resource commitment (stage models of internationalization) or high control modes (internalization theory).

From the late 1980's on, *the new venture literature* has addressed small firms that operated internationally early in their existence despite limited resources and capabilities (Sharma/Johanson 1987, Welch/Luostarinen 1988, McDougall 1989, Oviatt/McDougall 1994, McDougall et al. 1994, Bell 1995, Knight/Cavusgil 1996, Coviello/Munro 1997, Madsen/Servais 1997, Oviatt/McDougall 1999, Schrader et al. 2000). Oviatt and McDougall (1994) define such international new ventures as firms that from their inception seek to derive significant competitive advantage from the use of resources from and sales of outputs in multiple countries. Theoretical explanations offered for accelerated internationalization emphasize the increasing importance of network relations, industrial conditions, manager/entrepreneur's capabilities and mind set, and, perhaps, most importantly technological change (Oviatt/McDougall 1999, Knight/Cavusgil 1997) relative to difficulties of acquiring foreign market knowledge. Even though a theoretical framework that comprehensively addresses accelerated internationalization of new ventures, typically, small firms is lacking (Madsen/Servais 1997, Oviatt/McDougall 1999), theoretical buildings blocks and explanations have emerged that contribute to understanding accelerated internationalisation patterns across countries.

In the following, we consider explanations offered by the internationalisation, internalisation, and new venture literature regarding entry mode and internationalisation patterns and contrast them with the internationalisation process of eBay.

Entry Choices in Single Foreign Markets

A key reason that accounts for the slow pace of increasing international resource commitment of physical good providers is as Forsgren and Johanson (1992, p. 10) note: International expansion [be it in a single markets or across markets] is inhibited by the lack of knowledge about markets. With regards to the internationalization process of eBay, the lack of foreign market knowledge that results in liability of foreignness seems to have mattered. For example, eBay conceded that it stumbled in executing its strategy in the market by not sufficiently adapting the eBay Japan site for the Japanese market. Customizing the site to the needs of Japanese users has been attempted: eBay wrote the content exclusively in Japanese and allowed users to bid in yen, and added categories with a local flavour (such as Hello Kitty, Pokemon and pottery). Likewise, difficulties in handling transactions in Europe with regards to debit collection have complicated international expansion. This is due to the fact that there is no shared European ACH-style network, and differing regulations in European nations despite the existence of the EU and the Euro. Nonetheless, while complications associated with liability of foreignness can be noted, there are also clear deviations between eBay's internationalization process and the theoretical implications that are suggested – both in current internationalization and internalization theory with regards to entry modes in single countries.

One implication of lacking foreign market knowledge suggested in internationalization theory is, as authors (Johanson/Wiedersheim 1975, Johanson/Vahlne 1990) argue, that foreign market penetration in a single market follows a path of increasing commitment from no regular export activities through export by agents and licensing agreements to the more commitment intensive establishment of sales subsidiaries, joint ventures and overseas production units. As experimental knowledge about particular markets accumulates, internationalization theory suggests that risk exposure is attenuated and firms do escalate their resource commitments from low to high investment intensive foreign entry modes. In other words, if there is lacking knowledge about foreign markets, firms limit their risk exposure through limiting resource commitments. While individual resource commitment to particular foreign markets may require less investment for eBay (it takes little more than setting up a few computers, install the software, and leverage a brand) compared to physical good providers (which may require to set up production facilities, buying land etc.), entry modes chosen by eBay hardly correspond to theoretical predictions of internationalization literature. eBay entered the market in the UK (through Greenfield investments), and Australia (through an alliance) during 1999, it also entered almost simultaneously the German market (through acquisition). Later, market presence has been established simultaneously in Canada (through Greenfield), Japan (through a joint venture), and France (Greenfield followed by acquisition) during 2000. Korea followed in 2001 (through acquisition). Japan has been exited and Taiwan was entered (through acquisition) in 2002.

The internalization literature is complementary to the internationalization literature in its concern with single entry mode decisions in particular foreign markets, but it is mainly based on transaction cost economics (Williamson 1975, Caves 1982, Hymer 1976, Casson 1982). Like stage models of internationalization, it is suggested that a lack of foreign market knowledge, including local habits, business rules, and language is likely to increase risk exposure in international expansion resulting in 'liability of foreignness.'[7] However, unlike internationalization process theory which suggests that risk exposure might be controlled by limiting resource commitments[8] until foreign market knowledge has been acquired, internalization theory stresses the possibility to control expropriation risks[9] through internalizing *vertical activities* required to do business in foreign locations (e.g. Kogut 1988, Teece 1976, Kogut/Zander 1995, McFetridge 1995).[10]

For example, liability of foreignness can cause a relative disadvantage vis-a-vis locally established firms because the entrant faces higher (perhaps prohibitive) coordination costs compared to companies transacting within, rather than across, country borders. The entrant may compensate temporary disadvantages of foreignness by other advantages including proprietary knowledge, knowledge sharing systems, reputation and brands among other things (Buckley/Casson 1976). However, if it is difficult to trade such assets in spot transactions or craft licensing agreement with host country partners in vertical relations, for example, due to market failures or imperfection (Teece, 1976, Kogut/Zander 1995, McFetridge 1995), firms may take resort to entry modes that allow hierarchical control, including FDI (Casson 1982, 1999, Dunning 1988).[11] Casson (1999) adds that to the extent the MNC can more credibly convey quality assurance through branding relative to a host country partner, internalization of activities may also help customers overcome uncertainty about the good in question through direct contracting with the original supplier.[12] In sum, the less property right and strategic protection against misappropriation of rents to intangible assets such as brands and reputation by foreign contracting partners is possible, and the more important such assets are for signaling quality, the more firms will tend to international expansion by FDI (e.g. via merger & acquisitions and Greenfield investments) for reasons of control. Consequently, entry modes chosen by the internationalizing firm rests on the costs and benefits of alternative governance arrangements with firms seeking to minimize transaction costs that in turn depend on degree of foreign market knowledge.[13] The predictions of internalization theory are partially supported in the eBay case, as liability of foreignness can be assumed to be high in Germany, France, Korea, and Taiwan where eBay entered through high control modes. On the other hand, where liability of foreignness can be assumed to be relatively low such as in the UK and Canada, eBay choose to enter via high control modes as well. Thus, eBay entered through high control modes in both groups (high vs. low liability of foreignness).

In sum, the proposition that internationally expanding firms choose entry modes to minimize transactional risks that are associated with lacking foreign market knowledge (internalization theory) or controls for foreign country risks through limiting resource exposure until market knowledge has been acquired (internationalization theory) is partially supported at best. This begs the question for alternative explanations regarding entry choices during international entry. Unfortunately, the new venture literature offers „. . .little understanding about why combinations (of particular entry modes) are chosen. . ." (Oviatt/McDougall 1999, p. 6).

International Expansion Patterns Across Country Markets

While early work in internalization theory was restricted to the internationalization path in a single market, Johanson and Vahlne (1977, 1990) expand the explanatory reach of the stage model to propose patterns of internationalization across a series of new geographic markets, that may particularly well apply to early stages of internationalization. To control for risks associated with lacking local 'market knowledge', firms may tend to enter foreign markets that are similar in culture, language, rules and norms, and business networks before they expand to foreign markets that are increasingly dissimilar. By implication, like in individual market entry decisions, it is through the gradual acquisition, integration and utilization of foreign market knowledge that firms become willing to successively increase commitments across foreign markets (Penrose 1959, Sharma 1997). To recall the internationalization pattern of eBay: The company entered the market in the UK, Australia, and Germany during 1999 followed by Canada, Japan, and France during 2000. Korea followed in 2001 (acquisition). Japan was exited, Taiwan, and China was entered in 2002. With regards to theoretical predictions, eBay's internationalization process started in the UK and Canada, e.g. countries with low psychic distance, but then rapidly moved to countries with greater psychic distance such as Germany, Japan, France, and Korea. So we are entitled to expect that the internationalization path of digital information good providers may be driven by other factors than those suggested in stage models of internationalization.

The international new venture literature addresses factors that contribute to the understanding of 'accelerated internationalization'. First, international ventures may reflect the adaptation of the Japanese *keiretsu model*, where the internationally expanding small firm in mature markets follows as dependent supplier a large international expanding firm (Dunning 1993, Johanson/Vahlne 1990). Second, even independent new ventures operating in niche markets may exhibit patterns of accelerated internationalization. If firms operate in niche markets or narrow product lines, growth objectives will be constrained by limited home demand (Luostarinen 1989). Accordingly, international expansion might provide the only growth path (Coviello/Munro 1997), internationalization may be required to achieve economies of scale (Buckley/Casson 1976, Dunning 1993), or to leverage differentiation advantages gained at home through foreign market expansion (e.g., Oviatt/McDougall 1994, Shrader et al. 2000). In the case of eBay none of these explanations seem to apply. First, eBay is not a dependent supplier which follows a global customer. It targets a mass market that is still growing domestically, rather than a local niche market contained home demand. So international expansion is not the only growth path. Finally, while economies of scale in production might be augmented through international expansion with regards to eBay's IT platform, eBay is hardly differentiated from other providers of online auctions with regards to product features, except for a powerful brand.

However, firms may also expand internationally as part of a network of personal and industrial relation. As argued by Coviello and McAuley (1999, p. 227), the network perspective draws on social exchange and resource dependence ideas to suggest that „...internationalization depends on an organization's set of network relationships rather than specific company advantages." By implication, to view a firm's international expansion process as independent from other industry players and personal relations to international networks might be misleading.

Johanson and Mattsson (1988) argued that firms seek to obtain a position in an industrial value network. If an industrial network is already internationally developed, an international 'late starter' firm may be able to draw on complementary resources through joint ventures and tap more readily into established international industrial networks. Hence, international expansion may proceed faster, compared to firms that operate in industries where international industry networks have not been established yet. Such networks may well be instrumental for firms for rapid internationalization because networks often allow access complementary resources to compensate for lack of own capabilities and assets (Jolly et al. 1992, McDougall et al. 1994). Bell (1995) in study of 187 small software firms from Norway, Ireland, and Finland, suggest that networks and trends to cooperation rather than psychic distance contribute to explain internationalization patterns. Coviello and Munro's (1995, 1997) findings on small software firms point in the same direction: network relations are used to externalize market development activities.

In online auctions, eBay was an early starter that could not rely on industrial networks developed by others with one notable exception: during 1999 eBay forged a marketing deal with American Online (AOL), which placed eBay across AOL's domestic and international brands, such as AOL and CompuServe, the AOL.com Web page, and Netscape's Netcenter portal. Thus, eBay can create customized, co-branded sites across AOL's network. At the time of the agreement

AOL had established a local presence in the UK and Canada (1996), France (1996), Germany (1995), and Australia (1998) – all markets that eBay entered as well.

Personal international networks may also contribute to manager/entrepreneur's experience and open attitude. Furthermore, individual managers with an international mind set may have international access to social networks (e.g. Coviello/Munro 1997, Bell 1995, Oviatt/McDougall 1994). This, in turn, can contribute to early internationalization (Reuber/Fischer 1997, Knight/Cavusgil 1996). For example, Sharma and Johanson (1987) argue that network relations may 'become bridges to foreign markets.' If managers have acquired prior foreign market knowledge the internationally expanding firm may not need to acquire knowledge by itself, and one would expect faster internationalization and higher commitment modes. eBay's top management team might have contributed to its rapid internationalization process as well. For example CEO Meg Whitman acquired international experience in brand building during her prior employment at Walt Disney, Procter & Gamble, and Hasbro. Similarly, Matt Bannick, who lead market entry in France, and Korea acquired international experience at McKinsey. Thus one may well assume that, prior international experience might have contributed to accelerated internationalization.

In sum, the internationalization path across countries of eBay cannot be explained through lacking foreign 'market knowledge' alone, which leads the internationally expanding firm to enter foreign markets that are similar in culture, language, rules and norms, and business networks before they expand to foreign markets that are increasingly dissimilar. Explanations offered in the 'new venture literature' with regards to top-management's international orientation and utilization of international networks do contribute a possible explanation of eBay's rapid internationalization across countries. Case evidence is sparse, however. In the following section we seek to outline how considering product characteristics of digital information goods can contribute to explain international expansion both with regards to internationalization paths across countries and single market entry decisions.

Advancing Current Theory of International Expansion

The analysis in the previous section concluded that current theory only partially explains entry choice in single markets and internationalization patterns across markets of eBay although foreign liability due to lacking foreign market knowledge remains clearly important. This calls for refinement and extension of current literature. This article suggests advancing current theory by integrating product characteristics of digital goods as an important variable in the explanation of entry modes and internationalization patterns. The integration of product characteristics contributes to the understanding of international expansion in two ways. First, they modify existing predictions, and second, they suggest new predictions that cannot be reduced to arguments in the existing literature.

Single Market Entry Choice: The Influence of Digital Good Characteristics

Digital information good providers seek to enter foreign markets through entry modes that allow control in branding and advertising strategies that are necessary because of the experience character of digital information goods. While we have argued that liability of foreignness matters in the internationalization process of digital good providers, learning of customers about the products of the foreign firm may equally matter, and perhaps even more than learning of the firm about a particular market. Thus entry modes may be chosen to seek control regarding possibilities of customer education rather than overcoming the hazards of liability of foreignness. By implication, an advanced theory of international expansion benefits from recognising liability of foreignness as a bilateral concept: Both customers and the foreign entrant engage in learning during market entry. While building a brand is important for reasons of customer lock-in that facilitates network effects, and high control modes may be chosen accordingly, seeking high control modes through M&A may also lead to a dilemma for digital information good providers such as eBay. By gaining control, competitors are eliminated that may be instrumental to educate customers about innovative product and services during the creation of new international markets.

While the product characteristics based predictions regarding high control modes may coincide with predictions taken from internalization theory when liability of foreignness is high (which makes contractual hazards a more likely case), our argument must not refer to expropriation hazards that are due to liability of foreignness in vertical relations. Instead, when choosing high control modes in markets for digital information goods that exhibit, for example, low liability of foreignness (which makes expropriation hazards a less likely case), the internationally expanding firm might want to keep control over branding, because customer learning that is facilitated by branding is crucial to succeed in the market. Thus, a theory of entry mode choice in single foreign markets that relates to digital good characteristics (e.g. experience good character, lock-in, and network effects) can explain why high control modes are chosen during market entry, even if there is low liability of foreignness and expropriation hazards are less of a concern.

An alternative explanation for high control modes is possible even if one concurs with the arguments of internalization theory that firms respond to expropriation hazards by internalizing transactions. Shrader et al. (2000) suggested recently that firms might trade-off risks associated with international expansion such as risks associated with liability of foreignness and the risk related to entry modes. Integrating a foreign firm into another organization is particularly tricky as suggested in the literature on post-merger integration (e.g. Capron et al. 1999). Thus the foreign entrant may compare transaction risks (which internalization theory addresses) with post-merger integration risks (that it neglects). Digital good characteristics influence this risk trade off, however, as digital information good providers operate in markets with demand side economies of scale. Where network effects are present, a late entrant in particular foreign market faces an additional risk trade-off: incurring post-merger integration risks or loosing the market completely on the other (witness the failed attempt of eBay to gain traction in Japan against the market leader Yahoo!). In fact, as a late entrant, it is hard to imagine how low commitment modes (e.g. licensing) may give access to an installed client base because the incumbent will either fight or sell the client base, most likely by selling the whole company. In sum, digital information good providers seek to penetrate foreign markets rapidly and through entry modes that allow them to reap economies of scale in production, to benefit from network effects, as well as to control branding.

In the analysis above we have also noted that international entry of eBay in single country markets does not follow an incremental process of increasing commitment as market uncertainties are resolved through the acquisition of local market knowledge as suggested in internationalisation theory. To be sure, the new venture literature suggests, as was the case with eBay, that a management team that has acquired foreign market knowledge up front, may make more commitment intensive entry modes possible. In other words: learning about foreign markets takes place before a focal company engages in international expansion. A complementary explanation has to do, of course, with the already above discussed network effects, but, in addition one characteristic of digital information goods alters predictions of current internationalization theory: possibilities of cheap learning about customer preferences for product adaptation after market entry. When costs of gathering customer data and learning about customer preferences are low in comparison to physical good providers, liability of foreignness becomes less of an issue in retarding resource commitment. This is because it can be faster and cheaper dealt with through new methods of learning that a digital good provider can use to greater extend than a physical good provider.

Moreover, required resource commitment in absolute value may be less for digital good providers compared to physical good providers, at least as far a Greenfield investment is concerned (e.g. high control and high commitment mode). Note in this context, that control to achieve transaction efficiency may be associated with high resource commitment (e.g. M&A or Greenfield) as suggested in internationalization theory, but this is not always the case. First, as far as digital information good providers are concerned, high control modes may not coincide with high resource commitments. Market entry for a digital information good provider may mean no more than to buy a domain name, hire some marketing people, and set up servers that run local traffic. Second, there are substitutes for ownership in achieving control such as network governance (e.g. Holmstrom/Roberts 1998, Larsen 1992) during international market entry. Greenfield investments and M&A may also require less resource commitment relative to joint ventures with opportunistic or incapable partners in foreign markets – at least in the long run (e.g. Prahalad/Hamel 1990.)

Digital Product Characteristics and Patterns of Firms' Expansion Across Markets

Digital information good providers seem to deviate from a slow and incremental international expansion process across countries. As suggested in the new venture literature, they seek to create value abroad early in their existence (Oviatt/McDougall 1994). The explanations offered for 'accelerated internationalization' in the 'new venture literature' regarding prior experience of the management team, as well as possible co-operations with network partners have played a role in our case illustration. However, including product characteristics of digital information goods in the analysis of accelerated internationalization provides additional force to recent arguments that technological change and its implications become relatively more important relative to risk arguments that relate to the slow acquisition of tacit market knowledge. With regards to the increasing importance of technological advance relative to tacit foreign market knowledge (Oviatt/McDougall 1999), our analysis of digital information goods suggests that foreign market entry across countries may proceed more rapidly than those of physical good providers. This is because post-entry product adaptations are possible and exhibit low costs. As was the case with single market entry mode choices, where learning for local adaptation can be achieved cheaply and rapidly through gathering data about customer preferences, the retarding force of lacking market knowledge is weakened both in a single, but also across foreign markets.

While transportation costs matter for digital information good providers, they matter far less compared to physical good providers. Digital information costs have lower costs of transportation compared to physical goods, their providers need not be very selective with choices of in-market locations. Issues of storing, inventory management and logistics are of little concern to digital information good providers when making location decisions. Thus, liability of foreignness might be less pronounced regarding such issues.

Digital information good providers, such as eBay, seem to select foreign markets for entry that have high Internet penetration and advanced telecommunication infrastructures. This is because the availability and costs of such complimentary services influence the demand of digital goods providers. For example,

Canada, Germany, and Korea have well developed infrastructures that allow a strongly growing customer base to participate in online auction. So what may look as random patterns of market selection in the internationalization path of eBay, might be strongly influenced by available infrastructure and its costs to users in selected countries. In other words, international expansion across countries is driven by market selection according to market size and growth, which is effectively constrained by costs and possibilities to access the services of digital information good providers. By implication, digital information good providers seek to enter foreign markets first that have high Internet penetration and advanced telecommunication infrastructures (e.g. providers of complementary assets).

Moreover, as argued above, building brands for new categories of digital information goods, while crucial in markets where information costs are high, is also expensive. Online-auction provision constitutes a new industry and where no strong local brands existed, there was little possibility for eBay but to build a brand and create a market on its own. However, in markets where strong local competitors have already created a market for online auctions, as was the case in Germany, France, Korea, and Taiwan, the possibility for eBay to take advantage of high share prices to enter the market via mergers may have been the best option to gain market leadership despite the obvious difficulties of entering a foreign market as a second mover. In other words, saving on costs of market development and buying into the business of the first mover who has already an installed customer base, might have driven market selection in the case of eBay far more than concerns that relate to the liability of foreignness. In sum, psychic distance matters less when digital good providers select markets according to market size and growth, complementary infrastructure investments by others, competitor presence during market development, and availability of strong acquisition targets that allow brand leverage due to a large installed customer base. These factors may be far more important to achieve network effects and economies of scale in production in particular markets that the digital good provider might want to serve.

Finally, while the market for online auctions seems to develop rapidly as more and more countries provide for needed complementary infrastructure at low costs, market development does not work with the same pace across all foreign countries. Particular markets may be selected as an option and bridgehead for further expansion when a local provider (e.g. iBazar in France, Internet Auction in Korea) that eBay purchased engaged in market development activities in countries that will develop to full market size once market development becomes less constrained due to lacking infrastructure, customer learning, or Internet penetration. Seen this way, the internationalization path of eBay looks less random. Market selection is driven by option values that are associated with an installed base of customers as well as the possibility to expand into third countries.

Conclusions

The paper illustrates and advocates the integration of good characteristics in general and digital information good characteristics (experience good character, transportation costs, (re-) production-, and product adaptation costs) in particular as an important element in the explanation of international expansion. It develops theory to propose how considering digital good characteristics modifies and extends existing explanations with regard to entry mode choices (in single markets) and internationalization path (across countries). Explanations offered relate to network effects, lock-in, complementary infrastructure investments, branding and customer learning that are particularly pronounced in international markets for digital information goods. Thus, the paper contributes to advance a more comprehensive and contextually sensitive theory of the internationalizing firm that is especially relevant for companies that seek to take advantage of technological advance through the provision of digital information goods. The paper demonstrates how the explanations of stage models of internationalization, internalization theory, and international new venture research relate to the internationalization of digital information good providers. An explorative case study on eBay's internationalization process served as context for theory development to illustrate the need for, and possibilities of, integrating product characteristics of digital information goods in particular. However, eBay is a pure digital information good provider, but many companies build their business by packaging digital information goods and physical elements in the services they offer (e.g. book retailing, banking etc). A crucial question for future empirical research actively pursue is therefore how mixed good characteristics influence the internalization process of the expanding firm.

Endnotes

1. Such companies may be called 'born global' (Knight/Cavusgil 1996), 'global start up' (Oviatt/McDougall 1994), 'high technology start up' (Jolly et al. 1992), or 'international new ventures' (McDougall et al. 1994). Here we adopt the latter term: 'international new venture' (INV).
2. Recently, scholars have begun to address challenges of the internationalizing service firm in greater depth (Buckley et al. 1992, Robert 1999). Although digital information goods share at times product features with services such as intangibility and experience good character, digital information goods do not require simultaneity of production and consumption (separability), are signified by high fixed and low marginal costs, which is not the case for many service products, and in contrast to many services they can be stored (non-perishability).
3. While we lack the benefits of historical hindsight as the internationalization process of the digital good provider eBay is still ongoing and evolving, our objective is to identify and illustrate

crucial product-characteristics that influence, eventually modify, and possibly extend explanations offered in the current international expansion literature. Yin (1994) argues that explorative case studies are particular adequate when 'how' and 'why' questions are addressed and theoretical advance may be expected from unique and contemporary events over which the investigator has little or no control (Yin 1994). The case is built from several semi-structured interviews with company representatives and secondary sources, such as the company's annual reports, press releases, as well as investment reports from UBS Warburg (23/1/01), Wassertein Parella (2/7/01), and Morgan Stanley Dean Witter (24/9/98). Nonetheless, the case in the current context serves as context for developing theoretical arguments only.

4 By implication, we are concerned with service providers such as Yahoo!, eBay, or AOL that have no direct involvement in the provision of physical goods. While many service providers may offer mixed goods combining digital goods with physical aspects (e.g. Amazon), for the moment being we focus on pure plays only.
5 Conversely, Aharoni (1996) finds one of the biggest differences between a physical good and a service is the fact that services very often are based on human resources (people-intensive) and in general they demand minimal investment in fixed assets.
6 See for a critical review of stage models and entry modalities (e.g. Andersen 1993, Melin 1992, Pedersen/Petersen 1998).
7 Main indicators used in the empirical literature on the liability of foreignness are: (a) elapsed time of operations in the foreign market (e.g. Zaheer/Mosakowski 1997, Barkema et al. 1996), (b) international experience of the entrant firm (Erramilli 1991, Forsgren/Johanson 1992), and (c) lack of knowledge about foreign markets.
8
9 These may be due to market imperfection that result from e.g. liability of foreignness in intermediate product markets.
10 Note that transaction cost theory in Williamson's (1985, 1996) version is generally concerned with vertical value chain relations where incentive alignment problems in the face of asset specific investments is the key concern. Broader versions of information/transaction costs (Coase 1937, Casson 1982) may equally be applied to both horizontal and vertical entry mode decisions.
11 Licensing agreements involving knowledge-based assets are often less desirable when MNCs enter new markets, for three reasons: (1) they may result in leakage of competitive knowledge to host country partners, (2) the licensing firm might loose strategic control and flexibility, and (3) the underlying knowledge might be only imperfectly transferred to the licensee because managerial know how cannot be perfectly codified (e.g. Winter 1987) causing the licensees not to exploit such knowledge to the same extent that the originating company could (e.g. Kogut/Zander 1995, Buckley/ Casson 1976).
12 Think of the successful branding strategies of fast food chains. The greater the uncertainty and distrust surrounding international business, the more managers may seek control through internalizing transaction (Coase 1937). Accordingly, to leverage its brand internationally, McDonald's owns its restaurants in Moscow but runs restaurants in New York City by franchising. In other words: by pooling ownership, incentives to haggle, cheat, and default are reduced.
13 Dunning (1988) adds that commitment intensive entry modes including FDI may be explained not only through ownership advantages of the MNC and opportunities of internalisation in intermediate product markets, but additionally through location advantages of the host country that serve to induce international expansion. By location advantages, Dunning means the possibility of using resource endowments that are specific to a particular location. Firms might want to tap into local knowledge sources, exploit low labour costs, or take advantage of physical resources. If managers believe that location advantages can beneficially be combined with firm specific capabilities such as technological skills, reputation, and know how, and the latter are difficult to exchange as argued above, then firms may be required to engage in FDI.

Literature

Aharoni, Y., Globalization of Professional Business Services, in: Aharoni, Y. (ed.), *Coalitions and Competition: The Globalization of Professional Business Services*, London: Rutledge Press 1996, pp. 1–19.
Andersen, O., On the Internationalization Process of Firms: A Critical Analysis, *Journal of International Business Studies*, 24, second quarter 1993, pp. 209–231.
Arrow, K., Economic Welfare and the Allocation of Resources of Invention, in Lamberton, D. M. (ed.), *The Economics of Communication and Information*., Cheltenham, UK: Edward Elgar 1997.
Bakos, Y./Brynjolfsson, E., Bundling Information Goods: Pricing, Profits and Efficiency, *Management Science*, 45, 12, 1999, pp.1613–1630.
Bakos, Y./Brynjolfsson, E., Bundling and Competition on the Internet, *Marketing Science*, 19, 1, 2000, pp. 63–82.
Barkema, H. G./Bell, J. H./Penning, J. M., Foreign Entry, Cultural Barriers, and Learning, *Strategic Management Journal*, 17, 2, 1996, pp. 151–66.
Bell, J., The Internationalization of Small Computer Software Firms – A Further Challenge to „Stage" Theories, *European Journal of Marketing*, 29, 8, 1995, pp. 60–75.
Brynjolfsson, E./Kahin, B., *Understanding the Digital Economy*, Cambridge, MA: MIT Press 2000.
Buckley, P. J., & Casson, M., *The Future of the Multinational Enterprise*, New York: Holmes & Meier 1976.
Buckley, P. J./Pass C. L./Prescott K., The Internationalization of Service Firms: A Comparison with the Manufacturing Sector, *Scandinavian International Business Review*, 1, 1, 1992, pp. 39–56.
Caves RE., *Multinational Enterprise and Economic Analysis*, Cambridge, UK: Cambridge University Press 1982.
Capron, L./Hulland, J., Redeployment of Brands, Sales Forces and Marketing Expertise Following Horizontal Acquisitions: A Resource-based View, *Journal of Marketing*, 63, 1999, pp. 41–54.
Casson, M., Transaction Costs and the Theory of Multinational Enterprise, in Rugman A. M. (ed.), *New Theories of the Multinational Enterprise*, New York: St. Martin's Press 1982.
Casson, M. C., The Organization and Evolution of the Multinational Enterprise: An Information Cost Approach, *Management International Review*, 39, 3, 1999, pp. 77–121.
Coase, R. H., The Nature of the Firm, *Economica*, 4, 1937, pp. 386–405.
Coviello, N./McAuley A., Internationalization of the Smaller Firm: A Review of Contemporary Empirical Research, *Management International Review*, 39, 3, 1999, pp. 223–256.
Coviello, N. E./Munro, H. J., Growing the Entrepreneurial Firm: Networking for International Market Development, *European Journal of Marketing*, 29, 7, 1995, pp. 49–61.
Coviello, N./Munro, H., Network Relationships and the Internationalization Process of Small Software Firms, *International Business Review*, 6, 4, 1997, pp. 361–386.
Cyert, R. D./March, J. G., *A Behavioral Theory of the Firm*, , Englewood Cliffs, NJ: Prentice-Hall 1963.
Davenport, T. H./Beck, J. C., Getting the Attention You Need, *Harvard Business Review*, September–October 2001, pp. 119–126.
Dixit, A. K./Nalebuff, B. J., *Thinking Strategically: The Competitive Edge in Business, Politics, and Everyday Life*, New York: W. W. Norton 1991.
Dunning, J., The Eclectic Paradigm of International Production: A Restatement and Some Possible Extensions, *Journal of International Business Studies*, 19, 1, 1988, pp.1–31.
Dunning, J. H., The Changing Dynamics of International Production, in: Dunning, J. H. (ed.), *The Globalization of Business*, Rutledge: London and New York 1993, pp. 51–77.
Erramilli, M. K., The Experience Factor in Foreign Market Entry Behaviour of Service Firms, *Journal of International Business Studies*, 22, 3, 1991, pp. 479–501.
Forsgren, M./Johanson, J., *Managing Networks in International Business*, Philadelphia: Gordon and Breach 1992.
Holmström, B./P. Roberts., The Boundaries of the Firm Revisited, *Journal of Economic Perspectives*, 12, 4, 1998, pp. 73–94.

Hymer, S. H., *The International Operations of National Firms: A Study of Direct Foreign Investment*, Cambridge, MA: The MIT Press 1976.

Johanson, J./Mattson, L. G., Internationalization in Industrial Systems- a Network Approach, in Hood, N. (ed.): *Strategies for Global Competition,* London: Croom Helm 1988.

Johanson, J./Wiedersheim-Paul E., Internationalization of the Firm – Four Swedish Cases, *Journal of Management Studies*, 8, 2, 1975, pp. 305–22.

Johanson, J./Vahlne J. E., The Internationalization Process of the Firm – a Model of Knowledge Development and Increasing Foreign Market Commitments, *Journal of International Business Studies*, 8, 1 1977, pp. 23–32.

Johanson, J./Vahlne, J.-E., The Mechanism of Internationalization, *International Marketing Review*, 7, 4, 1990, pp. 11–24.

Jolly, V. K./Alahuhta, M./Jeanette, J. P., Challenging the Incumbents: How High-Technology Start-ups Compete Globally, *Journal of Strategic Change*, 1, 1992, pp. 71–82.

Katz, M. L./Shapiro, C., Network Externalities, Competition and Compatibility, *American Economic Review*, 75, 1985, pp. 424–440.

Knight, G./Cavusgil, S. T., The Born Global Firm: A Challenge to Internationalization Theory, *Advances of international Marketing*, JAI Press 1996.

Knight, G./Cavusgil, S. T., Emerging Organizational Paradigm for International Marketing: The Born Global firm, paper presented at the Annual Meeting: *Academy of International Business*, Honolulu, HI 1997.

Kogut, B., The Effect of National Culture on the Choice of Entry Mode, *Journal of International Business Studies*, 19, 3, 1988, pp. 411–433.

Kogut, B./Zander, U., Knowledge, Market Failure and the Multinational Enterprise: A Theoretical Note, *Journal of International Business Studies*, 26, 2, 1995, pp. 399–408.

Larsen, A., Network Dyads in Entrepreneurial Settings: A Study of the Governance of Exchange Relationships, *Administrative Science Quarterly*, 37, 1992, pp.76–104.

Lieberman, M. B./Montgomery, D. B., First-Mover (Dis) Advantages: Retrospective and Link with the Resource-based View, *Strategic Management Journal*, 19, 1998, pp. 1111–1125.

Liebowitz, S. J./Margolis, S. E., Path Dependence, Lock-in, and History, *Journal of Law, Economics and Organization*, 7, 1995, pp. 205–226.

Lippman, S. A./Rumelt, R. P., Uncertain Irritability: An Analysis of Inter-firm Differences in Efficiency Under Competition, *Bell Journal of Economics*, 23, 1982, pp. 418–438.

Luostarinen, R., The Internationalization of the Firm., Helsinki: *Acta Academic Oeconomicae Helsingiensis* 1989.

Madsen, K./Servais, P., The Internationalization of Born Globals: An Evolutionary Process?, *International Business Review*, 6, 1997, pp. 561–583.

McDougall, P. P., International Versus Domestic Entrepreneurship: New Venture Strategic Behavior and Industry Structure, *Journal of Business Venturing*, 4, 1989, pp. 387–399.

McDougall, P. P., Explaining the Formation of International New Ventures: The Limits of Theories From International Business Research, *Journal of International Business Venturing*, 9, 1994, pp. 469–487.

McDougall, P. P., Shane, S./Oviatt, B. M., Explaining the Formation of International New Ventures: The Limits of Theories From International Business Research, *Journal of Business Venturing*, 9, 1994, pp. 469–487.

McFetridge, D. G., Knowledge, Market Failure, and the Multinational Enterprise: A Comment, *Journal of International Business Studies*, 26, 2, 1995, pp.408–422.

Nelson, R. R., Information and Consumer Behavior, *Journal of Political Economy*, May 1970, pp. 311–329.

Ostry, S., Technology, Productivity and the Multinational Enterprise, *Journal of International Business Studies*, 29, 1, 1998, pp. 85–99.

Oviatt, B. M./McDougall, P. P., Toward a Theory of International New Ventures, *Journal of International Business Studies*, 25, 1, 1994, pp.45–64.

Oviatt, B. M./McDougall, P. P., Global Start-ups: Entrepreneurs on a Worldwide stage, *Academy of Management Executive*, 9, 2, 1995, pp. 30–44.

Oviatt, B. M./McDougall, P. P., Challenges for Internationalization Process Theory: The case of International New Ventures, *Management International Review*, 37, 2, 1997, pp. 85–99.

Oviatt, B. M., McDougall, P. P., A Framework for Understanding Accelerated International Entrepreneurship, in Wright, R. (ed.), *Research in Global Strategic Management,* Stamford, CT: JAI Press 1999, pp.23-40

Penrose, Edith T., *The Theory of the Growth of the Firm,* Oxford: Basil Blackwell 1995.

Prahald, C. K./Hamel, G., The Core Competence of the Corporation, *Harvard Business Review,* No. 66 1990.

Reuber, A. R./Fischer, E., The Influence of the Management Team's International Experience on the Internationalization Behaviors of SMEs, *Journal of International Business Studies,* 28, 1997, pp. 807-825.

Roberts, J., The Internationalization of Business Service Firms: A Stages Approach, *The Service Industries Journal,* 4, 1999, pp. 68-88.

Rugman A. M., *Inside the Multinationals: The Economics of Internal Markets,* New York: Columbia University Press 1981.

Rumelt, R. P./Lippman, S. A., Uncertain Irritability: An Analysis of Inter-firm Differences in Efficiency Under Competition, Bell Journal of Economics, 23, 1982, pp. 418-438.

Shrader, R., How New Ventures Exploit Trade-offs Among International Risk Factors: Lessons for Accelerated Internationalization of the 21st Century, *Academy of Management Journal,* 43, 6, 2000, pp. 1227-1247.

Sharma, D. D./Johanson, J., Technical Consultancy in Internationalization, *International Marketing Review,* 1987, pp. 20-29.

Teece, D. J., Transactions Cost Economics and the Multinational Enterprise: An Assessment, *Journal of Economic Behavior and Organization,* 7, 1986, pp. 21-45.

Varian H./Shapiro, V., *Information Rules,* Cambridge, MA: HBR Press 1999.

Welch, L./Luostarinen, R., Internationalization: Evolution of a Concept, *Journal of General Management,* 14, 2, 1981, pp. 34-55.

Williamson, O. E., *Markets and Hierarchies: Analysis and Antitrust Implications,* New York: Free Press 1995.

Williamson, O. E., Competitive Economic Organization: The Analysis of Discrete Structural Alternatives, *Administrative Science Quarterly,* 36, 1991, pp.269-296.

Winter, S., Knowledge and Competence as Strategic Assets, in Teece, D. (ed.), *The Competitive Challenge,* Cambridge, MA: Ballinger 1987, pp. 159-184.

Yin, R. K., *Case Study Research: Design and Method, revised edition,* California: Sage Publications 1989.

Zaheer, S./Mosakowski, E., The Dynamics of the Liability of Foreignness: G Global Study of Survival in Financial Services, *Strategic Management Journal,* 18, 6, 1997, pp. 439-464.

mir *Edition*

GABLER

Anja Schulte

The phenomenon of relocation
International location strategies of small and medium sized enterprises

2002, XX, 315 pages, pb., € 59,00 (approx. US $ 59,–)
ISBN 3-409-12375-X

The current German debate on globalisation is focussing mainly on enterprises leaving domestic locations and production sites. The small and medium sized enterprises (SMEs) that are relocating and concentrating their capacities back in their original home base have not received much attention. The author presents ten case studies that demonstrate the problems faced by the SME sector with respect to internationalisation and location strategies. An analysis is made of the requirements placed on SMEs and their activities in the context of the strong dynamics of internationalisation.

This book is aimed at researchers in the fields of international management, industrial sociology and SMEs, as well as SME managers and business consultants.

Betriebswirtschaftlicher Verlag Dr. Th. Gabler GmbH, Abraham-Lincoln-Str. 46, 65189 Wiesbaden

Management International Review

Neuerscheinungen

Joachim Scholz
Wert und Bewertung internationaler Akquisitionen
2001
XXII, 365 S. mit 40 Abb.,
(mir-Edition),
Br. € 79,–
ISBN 3-409-11602-8

Joachim Wolf
Strategie und Struktur 1955–1995: Ein Kapitel der Geschichte deutscher nationaler und internationaler Unternehmen
2000
XXXII, 673 S. mit 156 Abb.,
7 farb. Abb. (mir-Edition),
Br. € 94,50
ISBN 3-409-11637-0

Dodo zu Knyphausen-Aufseß (Hrsg.)
Globalisierung als Herausforderung der Betriebswirtschaftslehre
2000
XVIII, 285 S. (mir-Edition),
Br. € 64,–
ISBN 3-409-11719-9

Laila Maija Hofmann
Führungskräfte in Europa. Empirische Analyse zukünftiger Anforderungen
2000
XXVIII, 414 S. mit 89 Abb.,
129 Tab., Diss. Augsburg 2000
(mir-Edition),
Br. € 64,–
ISBN 3-409-11704-0

Frank Niederländer
Dynamik in der internationalen Produktpolitik von Automobilherstellern
2000
XXVIII, 296 S. mit 111 Abb.,
36 Tab., Dissertation Eichstätt 2000
(mir-Edition),
Br. € 59,–
ISBN 3-409-11722-9

Jan Hendrik Fisch
Structure Follows Knowledge. Internationale Verteilung der Forschung und Entwicklung in multinationalen Unternehmen
2001
XXII, 247 S. mit 84 Abb., 10 Tab.
(mir-Edition),
Br. € 49,–
ISBN 3-409-11802-0

Betriebswirtschaftlicher Verlag Dr. Th. Gabler GmbH, Abraham-Lincoln-Str. 46, 65189 Wiesbaden

EDITORIAL OBJECTIVES

MANAGEMENT INTERNATIONAL REVIEW presents insights and analyses which reflect basic and topical advances in the key areas of International Management. Its target audience includes scholars and executives in business and administration.

EDITORIAL POLICY

MANAGEMENT INTERNATIONAL REVIEW is a refereed journal which aims at the advancement and dissemination of international applied research in the fields of Management and Business. The scope of the journal comprises International Business, Transnational Corporations, Intercultural Management, Strategic Management, and Business Policy.

MANAGEMENT INTERNATIONAL REVIEW stresses the interaction between theory and practice of management by way of publishing articles, research notes, reports and comments which concentrate on the application of existing and potential research for business and other organizations. Papers are invited and given priority which are based on rigorous methodology, suggest models capable to solve practical problems. Also papers are welcome which advise as to whether and to what extent models can be translated and applied by the practising manager. Work which has passed the practical test of successful application is of special interest to MIR. It is hoped that besides its academic objectives the journal will serve some useful purpose for the practical world, and also help bridging the gap between academic and business management.

PUBLISHING · SUBSCRIPTION · ADVERTISEMENTS

Published quarterly, fixed annual subscription rate for foreign countries: Individual subscription 108 Euro (approx. US$ 112.–), institutional subscription 212 Euro (approx. US$ 219.–), single copy 59 Euro – (approx. US$ 55.–). Fixed annual subscription rate for Germany: Individual subscription 99 Euro –, institutional subscription 206 Euro. Payment on receipt of invoice. Subscriptions are entered on a calendar basis only (Jan.–Dec.). Cancellations must be filed by referring to the subscription number six weeks before closing date (subscription invoice); there will be no confirmation. There may be 1 to 4 supplementary issues per year. Each supplementary issue will be sent to subscribers with a separate invoice allowing 25% deduction on the regular price. Subscribers have the right to return the issue within one month to the distribution company. – Subscription office: VVA, post-box 7777, D-33310 Gütersloh, Germany. Tel. 0049/(0)5241-801968/802891, Fax 809620. Distribution: Kristiane Alesch, Tel. 0049/(0)611/7878-359. Reader-Service: Britta Christmann, Tel. 0049/(0)611/7878-129, Fax 7878-423. Advertising office: Thomas Werner, Tel. 0049/(0)611/7878-138.
Editorial Department: Ralf Wettlaufer, Tel. 0049/(0)611/7878-234, e-mail: ralf.wettlaufer@bertelsmann.de. Annelie Meisenheimer, Tel. 0049/(0)611/7878-232. Production: Gabriele McLemore, Betriebswirtschaftlicher Verlag Dr. Th. Gabler GmbH, Abraham-Lincoln-Straße 46, D-65189 Wiesbaden, Tel. 0049/(0)611/7878-0, Fax 7878-400. Internet: Publisher http://www.gabler.de; Editor http://www.uni-hohenheim.de/~mir; Managing Director Dr. Hans-Dieter Haenel; Publishing Director Dr. Heinz Weinheimer; Senior Publishing Editor Claudia Splittgerber; Sales Manager Gabriel Göttlinger; Production Manager Reinhard van den Hövel. Produced by Druckhaus „Thomas Müntzer" GmbH, Bad Langensalza – Contributions published in this journal are protected by copyright.

Copyright © Gabler Verlag, Wiesbaden 2003.

Gabler Verlag is a company in the specialist publishing group BertelsmannSpringer.

No part of this publication may be reproduced, stored in a retrieval system or transmitted in any form or by any means: electronic, magnetic tape, mechanical, photocopying, recording or otherwise, without permission in writing from the publisher. There is no liability for manuscripts and review literature which were submitted without invitation.

ISSN 0938-8249

GPSR Compliance

The European Union's (EU) General Product Safety Regulation (GPSR) is a set of rules that requires consumer products to be safe and our obligations to ensure this.

If you have any concerns about our products, you can contact us on

ProductSafety@springernature.com

In case Publisher is established outside the EU, the EU authorized representative is:

Springer Nature Customer Service Center GmbH
Europaplatz 3
69115 Heidelberg, Germany